THE SPLENDID WAYFARING

THE
SPLENDID
WAYFARING

The story of the exploits and adventures of Jedediah
Smith and his comrades, the Ashley-Henry men, discoverers and explorers of the great Central Route from
the Missouri River to the Pacific Ocean, 1822–1831

John G. Neihardt

UNIVERSITY OF NEBRASKA PRESS · LINCOLN

First Bison Book printing: September 1970

*Bison Book edition published by arrangement with
John G. Neihardt.*

Manufactured in the United States of America

TO
MY GOOD COMRADE

JULIUS T. HOUSE

ζευχθεὶς ἕτοιμος ἦν ἐμοὶ σειραφόρος

PREFACE

The student of American History in our schools is given an opportunity to become well acquainted with the early explorations of the Great Northwest and the Great Southwest; he is taught little or nothing of the real discoverers of the central route from the Missouri River to the Pacific Ocean. This is due to the fact that, until very recently, our historians have been concerned too much with governmental acts, too little with the activities of the people themselves. The official explorers of the Northwest and the Southwest were actually pioneers; but the official exploration of the great central region beyond the Rockies was undertaken twenty years after the actual discoverers and explorers had set out from St. Louis. Considering the fact that it was by way of the central route that the tide of migration flowed across the Rockies and possessed the Far West, it would seem that the discovery and exploration of that route might now, at last, be given some attention in our schools.

In the following pages I have told the story of that body of adventurers who, from 1822 to 1829, opened the way for the expansion of our nation beyond the Missouri. I have made Jedediah Smith the central figure of my story, for of all explorers of the Great West he was in many ways the most remarkable, though, heretofore, our school children have not even heard his name. In order to give the student a sense of the continuity of history, I have begun my narrative with a brief account of the movement across the Alleghenies and down the Ohio River after the Revolutionary War; and I have suggested the relation of westward expansion in America to the whole race movement from the beginning.

The general mood of a given period is quite as important a part of history as are the bare facts. Therefore, by way of giving a more vivid picture of the times, I have taken the liberty to supply minor details in Chapters I, II, IV, V, VIII, IX, and X; but in every case I have done this strictly in accordance with the recorded experiences of contemporaries in similar situations. Also, as a matter of convenience in shaping the narrative, I have assumed that Smith went to St. Louis in the spring of 1822. There are good reasons for believing that this may be correct, though the year of his arrival there is unknown. In every other respect the narrative faithfully follows the chain of facts as found in the authentic sources.

Though I have drawn upon a considerable number of sources, as will be seen by consulting the bibliography at the back of the book, I am especially indebted to Prof. Dale's admirable work, " The Ashley-Smith Explorations," which not only clears up some important points in the history of the period, but presents for the first time certain recently discovered documents bearing upon the expeditions of William H. Ashley and Jedediah Strong Smith. I must also acknowledge the following debts: to Mr. Doane Robinson, secretary of the Historical Society of South Dakota, who, twelve years ago, revealed to me the wonderful life-story of Jedediah Smith, and who has been most generous in furthering my work; to Miss Stella M. Drumm, librarian of the Missouri Historical Society, and to Mr. William E. Connelley, secretary of the State Historical Society of Kansas, who have kindly furnished me with copies of source material placed in their keeping; to Mr. Frederick S. Dellenbaugh for permission to use pictures from his " Canyon Voyage "; and to Mr. Enos A. Mills, Dr. George Wharton James and Prof. S. H. Knight for photographs.

JOHN G. NEIHARDT.

Bancroft, Nebraska,
December, 1919.

CONTENTS

THE SPLENDID WAYFARING

I

DOWN THE OHIO

A N early April dawn was whitening over the
vast forests of Kentucky and Ohio, and here
and there, from an occasional log cabin in a clearing, hearth-smoke began to rise. Out of the dim
wilderness to the east the broad Ohio River, now
swollen with the spring floods, came swirling down
past the thriving little city of Cincinnati set
staunchly on a sunward slope. Already the city
had awakened; but no auto horns honked, no trol-
ley gongs clanged in the streets, and no whistle of
an approaching locomotive disturbed the hush of
the great valley. No railroad trains would arrive that day, nor for many a day thereafter.
Though steamboats were now no longer uncommon, yet the bulk of traffic was still carried on in
a primitive way. This proud little metropolis of
an immense teritory, fabulously rich in all those
material things that contribute to the happiness of
men, knew nothing of telephones and telegraphs,
or of any of those conveniences without which an
American city can no longer be conceived. And

yet, during the day that was coming, as for a generation past, this bustling town would play its rôle in one of the most tremendous adventures that our race has experienced.

What race and what adventures?

In order to suggest the answer to this question, let us begin at the beginning, far back in the dim centuries, scanning as rapidly as possible what is, for us of the Western World, the greatest of all stories.   Only thus can we sense the magnitude and significance of what we are about to witness; for there are no divisions in time, and history is to be conceived, not as a succession of periods limited by dates on the calendar, but rather as one continuous process.   Well then, thousands of years ago the Aryan or Indo-European Race, dwelling in the valley of the Euphrates, was seized with the wanderlust.   A portion of this people turned toward India.   With those we are not here concerned.   A portion turned toward the setting sun, and so began a journey that should continue for thousands of years and thousands of miles, to reach our own Pacific Coast during the 19th century.   Those westering peoples were our ancestors; American history properly begins with them; and we today are the rightful heirs of all the heroism and beauty and wisdom that have been developed in their age-long pilgrimage.   We are what we are because of what they experienced.

Now as those ancestors of ours pressed west-

ward, they underwent many changes, owing to
varying physical environment, to contact with
other peoples, and to that evolution of ideas which
is the natural result of experience in meeting the
difficulties of life. As we follow them in their
westward migration, we know them under the
guise of many nationalities, speaking as many different tongues, yet the main line of descent runs
clear. We might liken the ancient Aryan spirit to
a prairie fire driven by an east wind out of Mesopotamia and destined to burn across a world.
Now it flared up in Persia, and the gloom of the
Past is still painted with that flare. Now it was
a white radiance in Greece, the clear illumina-
tion of which still guides the feet of men. Now
it burned ruddily in Rome, spread around the
Mediterranean, and became as a golden noonday
to all the known world. Then it drove northward
and lit Europe with a succession of illuminations.
Now its glowing center was in the Empire of
Charlemagne, now in Spain under the great Philip,
now in France under the Grand Monarch, now in
England under Elizabeth. Though whipped by
cross-winds and freakish gusts, changing ever by
that upon which it fed, yet it was ever the same
flame, ever yearning westward — in its rear the
ashes of fallen empires, in its van the rising and
falling light of what was yet to be. At last, borne
as a torch by the discoverers and explorers of the
Western Hemisphere, that flame was rekindled in

our own Colonial history. Up the Mississippi from the Gulf of Mexico came the Spaniards. Up the St. Lawrence forged the French. Westward across the Alleghenies and down the Ohio went the English and the Germans and the Dutch and the Irish. And all these scions of an ancient race were to meet and mingle in the great central valley, pushing on and on by river route and prairie trail and mountain pass to the waters of the Pacific. Here in the western continent the wanderings of the widely dispersed peoples should end at last, and they were destined to become again one people.

Thus it was that, on that April morning in 1822, the frontier city of Cincinnati was sharing in a great adventure — no less an adventure than the conquest of a continent. For a generation past, yonder river had been more than a stream of water. It had become a veritable stream of men, urged westward by the home-hunger and the lure of wealth — impulses no less elemental than that which now flung the spring-floods seaward.

That morning at the city's water-front a clutter of boats, moored along the wagon-rutted landing, made clear in what manner the stream of men would flow that day. And what a variety of water craft! There lay an ungainly side-wheeled steamboat, already belching smoke. Nearby was a stately barge, as big as an Atlantic schooner of those days, requiring at least twenty-five men to work it up-stream. Yonder was a keelboat, long, slender, gracefully shaped, capable of bearing thirty tons of freight and formed in such a way that it might easily be poled, towed by the cordelle, or driven under sail, when the wind was favorable, over the shallow waters of the summer season. Here, again, was a Kentucky flatboat, commonly known as a "broadhorn." About fifteen feet wide and seventy-five feet long, it would carry at least sixty tons. It was like an ark adventuring toward some Ararat in the country of the sunset, for it bore a whole family with all its worldly goods — geese, chickens, horses, cows, sheep, pigs! And there were Allegheny skiffs, carrying from eight to twelve tons; pirogues, hollowed out of enormous trees; common skiffs, dugouts, and various nondescript boats displaying a whimsical combination of well known varieties.

Now there is a bustling, and a babble of voices, along the landing and among the cluttered craft. Neighborly messages are flung from deck to deck — pioneers of Kentucky hailing pioneers of the Mohawk Valley; Virginians and Pennsylvanians discussing hopes with adventurers from the Maumee or Sandusky Bay or Green River; traders with Yankee notions, tinware, pork, flour, hemp, tobacco, agricultural implements and Monongahela whisky for sale, question each other as to their cargoes and destinations among the Span-

ish and French settlements of the Mississippi.
And how oddly clad these people are! Every
member of yonder family on the Kentucky broadhorn is dressed in linsey, and it is a safe guess
that the mother, aided, perhaps, by the eldest
daughter, has scutched, heckled and spun the flax,
carded and spun the wool, woven and dyed the
cloth from which these garments were made.
Many of the men wear the hunting shirt, a large-
sleeved loose frock reaching half way between hip
and knee, open in front and wide enough to lap
over a foot or more when closed with the belt that
is tied in the back. A large cape, fringed, perhaps, with ravelled cloth of a gaudy color, falls
across the shoulders. Some of these shirts are
made of linsey, some of linen, some of dressed
deer skin. Breeches of buckskin, fringed at the
side seams, are common; and there are more moccasins among these adventurers than shoes.

The women, some of whom, no doubt, are destined to become the great grandmothers of some
of the proudest families of the West, have set off
their rude homespun garments with no more conspicuous adornment than a small hand-woven
handkerchief tied about the neck. Some are now
going barefoot, some wear moccasins, some the
coarsest of shoes. Few are the " store clothes "
to be noted among these people; and indeed, many
of them, reared in the backwoods, had perhaps
never seen a store until they came to stare at the

" sights " in Cincinnati, a huge metropolis to them.

Suddenly above the babble a boat horn strikes up a merry lilt. Others join in; and, far away, like spirit bugles out of the dim past of the race, still sounding the westward advance, the echoes sing on among the wooded hills. With a roar from her whistle the steamboat backs out, swings round, and, thrusting her stubborn nose into the swirl, pushes on toward Pittsburgh, snoring like an asthmatic sleeper. The cumbrous barge, poled by a dozen brawny men, moves slowly outward, feels the clutch of the current, and sweeps away. The ark-like broadhorn follows, while, startled by the shouting of the men and the blaring of the horns, the geese and chickens and sheep and cows and pigs and horses add each their own peculiar cries to the general din. And, indeed, why should they not be heard? Have they not shared as comrades in the age-long adventure of the race?

Skiffs, pirogues and dugouts are putting off. The keelboat's line is taken in; the patron, as the helmsman is called, is at the wheel; the crew makes ready to push off and join the flotilla, now swirling rapidly down the stream. The last passenger is going aboard — a slender, dark-haired young man of middle height, with an erect, alert bearing and a keenness of the eye that betokens resolution and intelligence. He must be well under twenty-five years of age. His clothes are of homespun and he carries upon his back a " plunder bag " doubtless containing all his worldly wealth. Let us follow him; for though yonder French boatman with his scarlet sash seems by far the more important person of the two, this young fellow, with the bag at his back, is fated to become one of the great torch-bearers of the race; and within nine years he shall have pushed far in advance of the oncoming human tide, discovered a main route of travel through the Western wilderness to the Pacific Ocean, encountered many perils, and died the death of a hero, leaving as a legacy to his countrymen the memory of his years, as rich as they were few.

Now the keelboat was in midstream, and soon the town was lost to view around a bend. Sitting on his " plunder bag " on the forward deck, the young man gazed dreamily at the two green worlds that flowed by him — a vision of universal fruitfulness. The magnificent beeches and sycamores and cottonwoods along the shore were in full leaf. Red birds flickered with mellow whistlings in and out among the dense foliage. Now and then a flock of paroquets shocked some green silence with eruptions of color and noise. Columns of smoke arose from occasional cabins in some hidden clearing beyond the dense wood that fringed the river. Ax-strokes, begetting multitudes of echoes, told where some lusty backwoodsman was contributing his share of labor to the making of a new world. Dogs barked far away, and echo dogs answered in the golden hush.

During the morning they had passed the mouth of the Great Miami on their right, and shortly afterward, the village of Lawrenceburg. Now and then a bend in the river revealed a patch of cleared ground wherein a barefooted plowman drove his team of oxen among the stumps; and then there arose a running fire of question and answer between the boats and the shore. The colloquy might run somewhat as follows:

" Hello, the boat! "

" Hello, the plow! Have you any potatoes to sell the boat? "

" None. Have you any whisky aboard the boat? "

" Plenty."

" Well, I'll trade potatoes for whisky."

" What do you ask for your potatoes? "

" A dollar a bushel."

" Too much."

" Well, I will let you have a bushel of potatoes for a gallon of whisky."

The boats move on.

" A half gallon! "

The voice grows dimmer with increasing distance.

" A quart! "

Or perhaps the conversation between boatmen and settler might call forth what passed for Yankee wit, as for instance:

Curious settler: " Where you from? "
Facetious boatman: " Redstone."
" What's your lading? "
" Millstones."
" What's the captain's name? "
" Whetstone."
" Where you bound? "
" Limestone." [1]
Sometimes, it is said, such dialogs between land and water developed into an exchange of blackguardly epithets, ending, as like as not, in the landing of the boatman and a brisk fight on shore. Nor should this greatly surprise us; for always at the lip of the advancing human flood the brawling and turbulent spirits are sure to be found; and indeed the race owes much to its wild and reckless types, for from their number have been recruited the rank and file of many a daring expedition into the wilderness, to the end that the way might be made clear for the home-makers. The race advances through its exceptions; that is to say, through those who refuse to think or act in accordance with established custom. Those, whose departures from what has been accepted as right prove at last to be advantageous to the race, become the great men and are justly honored. The others are overcome and forgotten. At one end of this scale of human exceptions we find the saint and seer; at the other end, the

[1] Flint. "Recollections of the Past Ten Years."

criminal. Many of those turbulent spirits that were of the greatest value in the pioneering age would, if confined to the uncongenial environment of a modern industrial city, end their days in a penitentiary.

The sun rose high above the drifting flock of boats and began the long descent of afternoon. Still the young man sat upon his " plunder bag " or paced about the keelboat's deck, dreamily watching the rich bottom lands and rolling hills drift past. No wonder that he had little heart for entering into the gay spirit of his fellow travellers. He was leaving home, and there was something inexorable about the swift and silent current that bore him farther and farther into a world unknown to him. And yet, there must have been a thrill in it all; for he had dreamed a daring dream of what a resolute young man might do in those vast, mysterious white spaces that then made up the greater portion of the map of the Trans-Missouri country. Doubtless, rivers and mountains and lakes had been waiting yonder for unknown ages for a white man to discover and name them! Might he not prove to be that white man? And beyond those vast white spaces lay the Pacific Ocean and the country of the Spaniards!

Seventeen years before, Lewis and Clark had pushed to the headwaters of the Missouri, across the mountains to the headwaters of the Columbia, and down that river to the sea.   But what of the way through the great country to the south? Who should find and plot it?

The setting sun glowed across the broad flood ahead, and the full moon rose huge and red through the mists of the valley in the rear.   It would be a white night; the high water made the river safe, and so the boats floated on into the deepening moony haze.   Suppers were cooked and eaten.   Then a squeaking fiddle struck up a familiar backwoods tune on board the Kentucky broadhorn.   Soon a dance was in full swing there, and the young men and women from the other boats were putting off in skiffs to join the merry-making.   Now and then bursts of song and shouts of laughter drowned out the clatter of heels and the shrill ecstasies of the racing fiddle.

But the young man, whom we have been noting, showed no inclination to join the merrymakers. He had been reading a book by the lingering twi-light, until the dusk had blotted out the dog-eared pages.   Then he had begun pacing up and down the deck, his head bowed, his hands clasped behind him; and, seen thus in the moonlight, he seemed more like an old man brooding upon the dead years, than a youth whose blood pulsed strongly with the lust of high adventure.   By and by the patron at the helm, a sturdy old graybeard from the Monongahela, hailed him:

"What book, young man? One of them love yarns, I'll warrant!"

"I was reading the Great Book, sir."

"Eh? — The Scriptures? A great book, indeed; and them as be kicking their heels in the devil's wind yonder might better be reading of it. Where bound?"

"To St. Louis."

"What you calc'late doing yonder?"

"I shall enter the fur trade."

"Aye, and go far, I'll warrant; for I see you be one of them as knows where they're going, keeps a tight lip and goes there by the grace of God! That breed goes far. Most ain't rightly sure where they be bound and never gets there — like me. My beard's gray and I be n't there yet, and so I know. Who be you, where you from, and who's your folks?"

Now even to the most taciturn and self-contained young man who is leaving home, that is likely to be a stimulating question, and the old patron got his answer. Our young hero's name was Jedediah Strong Smith. His father, Jedediah Smith, a native of New Hampshire, had pushed westward into the Mohawk Valley with the first wave of emigration after the close of the Revolutionary War, and had settled in Chenango County, New York. There in the village of Bainbridge, on June 24th, 1798, our hero was born.

But in spite of his large and growing family, the elder Smith had not long remained there, for the wanderlust of the race had been strong in him, and the lure of the sunset, that was to lead his son across the plains and mountains and deserts even to the waters of the Pacific, had led the father still farther to the west. For a few years the family had lived in Erie, Pennsylvania, and was now settled in Ashtabula, Ohio, with little prospect of moving any farther, for the children at home now numbered a baker's dozen.

Though the chances for education in the country of his childhood were slight in those days, Jed had been fortunate in making friends with a physician, Dr. Simons, who had given him the " rudiments of an English education and a smattering of Latin," together with a love for the Scriptures and the fear of God. At the age of thirteen, Jed had begun to shift for himself, having secured a job as clerk on one of the freight boats of the Great Lakes.[1] Thus at an impressionable age he had come in close contact with the traders and trappers of the British fur companies; and the many stirring tales he had heard from those adventurers had determined the course of his life. He too would brave the dangers of the wilderness! So now he was going to St. Louis, the great emporium of the American fur trade.

[1] Dale. " The Ashley-Smith Explorations."

The moon rose high, and still the old patron and the young adventurer talked of the Western Country, of St. Louis and of the bright prospects that the fur trade then offered to enterprising young men. At midnight the old man's watch ended, and another took the helm. Rolling themselves in their blankets, the graybeard and the youth lay down upon the forward deck to sleep. By and by the sound of merrymaking on the broadhorn trailed away into a great silence; and all night long the shadowy helmsmen, guiding the black hulks through mysterious immensity, " sailed astonished amid stars."

Boat horns called to the sleepers as the fleet drifted slowly out of the fading shadow into a new day. Once again neighborly voices were heard crying from deck to deck. The fleet was now drifting southwestwardly with the Indiana shore to starboard. Close on noon it passed the Kentucky River flowing bankfull out of the primeval forest to the southeast. Here a rude flatboat, that had been moored among the willows near the junction of the streams, put off and floated in among the other boats. It bore a large family with all its household goods, bound for the Wabash country — a fact which did not long remain a secret, for the meeting of pioneers involved no ceremony, and the father, who, with the aid of a lank, overgrown, frowsy-headed boy, guided his drifting home with a long sweep-oar at

the stern, was at once subjected to a running fire
of questions.

The course of the river shifted to the northwest, then to the west, then to the south.   Dusk
came, the moon rose.   All afternoon there had
been much talk of the Falls of the Ohio, now some
forty miles ahead, over which the fleet must pass.
Those who were travelling that way for the first
time naturally looked forward with dread to the
fancied dangers of the passage, though the old-
timers assured them that in high water there was
nothing to fear.   Nevertheless, in the wee hours
of the morning, the boats put in to shore, there
to await the dawn, that the falls might be passed
in daylight.

It was mid-forenoon when the lookout on the
leading boat, then drifting near Louisville in
waters as smooth as a lake, heard a deep roaring
ahead.   A cry of warning arose and spread over
the fleet, dying out suddenly as the first boat
rocked to the clutching swirl, leaped into a stretch
of wildly agitated waters and shot out into the
glassy quiet below.   It was all over in a few minutes; but when the boats once more drifted in
the dozing calm, the laughter of relaxing dread
and the pointless jests that were bandied from
deck to deck told how tense those minutes had
been.

There was now no obstacle to fear in the
whole course of the Ohio; and, favored by the

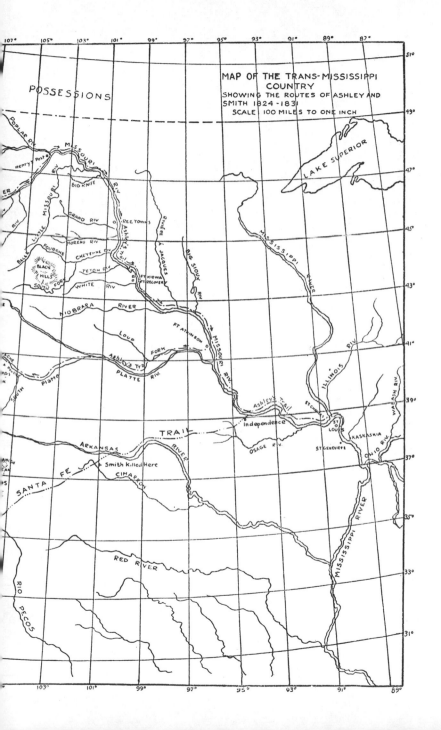

MAP OF THE TRANS-MISSISSIPPI
COUNTRY
SHOWING THE ROUTES OF ASHLEY AND
SMITH 1824-1831
SCALE 100 MILES TO ONE INCH

moon, the fleet continued to drift by night as well as by day, save when an occasional rainstorm darkened the sky. Now and then a stop was made at some settlement for the purpose of trading for supplies and getting acquainted. Some of the craft dropped out of the fleet at various points and others took their places. One day and night below the falls, they passed Blue River on their right. In three more days they saw Green River coming in out of Kentucky. Another day and night brought them to the mouth of the Wabash; and at noon of the following day they landed at Shawnee Town — an unpleasant looking little village, set upon low ground and now struggling with the flood waters. In spite of its appearance, however, it was then, and had been for years, a place of some importance, owing to the salt deposits nearby, which furnished its chief article of commerce, and to the fact that it had become an outfitting point for the Mississippi trade.

Here the keelboat which bore our hero took on nine French boatmen to aid in the difficult task of poling and cordelling from the mouth of the Ohio to St. Louis.

Now the river broadened; the bluffs began to fall away; cultivated patches became less frequent; dismal stretches of swamp land, haunted by water fowl, were more and more common. To right and left the lofty forests stretched away with a regular surface like a vast green roof supported by huge living columns rising out of the water. At rare intervals the solitary cabin of a wood cutter, set on piles or blocks to raise it above the inundation, served by contrast to make the scene more dismal.   A day and night from Shawnee Town the mouth of the Cumberland was passed; and a half day later, the Tennessee.   The next sunrise found them moored at the junction of the two great rivers.

Yonder magnificent stream was the Mississippi; and young Smith, gazing upon it for the first time, doubtless felt something of awe and the sense of losing a friendly world made dear with old associations, that the ancient Phœnician mariners must have experienced at the Pillars of Hercules.

Here at the delta speculators had once dreamed of founding a great commercial city, and a few houses had been raised on piles.   But the dream had failed, and now the town was kept on a huge flatboat a hundred feet long, in which there were stores, liquor shops, gambling dens, and a motley population of miserable men and women — a trap of vice for the unwary.   Here was the central point of the most extensive network of navigable rivers on the globe; a natural system of transportation that has not even now, at the end of the second decade of the twentieth century, been fully utilized to the advantage of mankind.   Keelboats and flat-bottomed mackinaws, starting at this point, could ascend to the headwaters of the

Mississippi; to the Great Falls of the Missouri in sight of the Rocky Mountains; to Pompey's Pillar on the Yellowstone; to the State of New York by way of the Ohio River; up the Illinois and down the Chicago to the Great Lakes; up the Wabash and the Tennessee into the heart of the great forests; or, descending to the Red River of the South or the Arkansas, it was possible to penetrate the great prairie wilderness of the Southwest even to the Spanish country.

Already the traffic that passed this point was immense, considering the undeveloped condition of the country. A short distance to the south, at the mouth of the Bayou, was the port of New Madrid; and there in a single spring day as many as a hundred boats had landed, laden with planks from the pine forests of southwestern New York; Yankee notions, corn in the ear, apples and potatoes from Ohio; pork, flour, whisky, hemp, tobacco, bagging and bale rope from Kentucky; cotton from Tennessee; cattle and horses from Missouri and Illinois. Sometimes a number of these craft would be lashed together, thus forming a floating town several acres in extent; and brisk was the trade and merry the festivities that were carried on in such drifting communities.

Now began the most difficult part of the voyage to St. Louis — a stretch of approximately two hundred miles against the full spring flood. The cordelle, or tow-line, swung from the masthead

of the keelboat, was flung ashore, and a dozen
boatmen, toiling tandem with the line across their
shoulders, began the long pull northward, while
the helmsman at the stern and a polesman at the
bow kept the craft well out in the stream.   Timothy Flint, an early traveller by keelboat up this
difficult stretch, has left us the following general
remarks regarding the labors and dangers attend-
ant upon such a voyage in those days: " Owing
to the character of the river and the numberless
impediments in it and on its banks, the cordelle is
continually entangling among the snags and saw-
yers between the boat and the shore, and has
often to be thrown over small trees and carried
around larger ones.   Sometimes you are impeded
by masses of trees that have lodged against saw-
yers.   At other times you find a considerable
portion of the shore, including a surface of acres,
that has fallen into the river with all its trees
upon it.   Just at the edge of these trees the current is so heavy as to be almost impassable.   It
is beside the question to think of forcing the boat
up against the main current anywhere, except with
an uncommon number of hands.   Therefore, any
impediment near the shore must either be sur-
mounted or the river crossed to avoid it.   It
often happens that the boat, with no small labor,
and falling down stream with the strength of the
current, crosses to avoid such difficulties and finds
equal ones on the opposite shore.   Sometimes you

are obliged to make your way among the trunks
of the trees, the water boiling round your boat
like a mill race. Then if the boat swings, you are
instantly carried back and perhaps strike the snags
below you, and your boat is staved. I do not remember to have traversed this river in any considerable trip, without having heard of some fatal
disaster to a boat, or having seen the dead body
of some boatman, recognized by the red flannel
shirt which they generally wear. The numbers of
carcasses of boats, lying at the points or thrown
up high and dry on the wreck heaps, demonstrate
how many are lost on this wild and, as the boatmen call it, wicked river." [1]

All day long, under such difficulties, with brief
but frequent breathing spells, the crew fought its
way up stream; and always the hardest task was
met with song, for the French boatmen were famous singers, peculiarly gifted with the genius
for light-heartedness. Often it became necessary
for all, save the helmsman, to take a hand in the
tense struggle with the sinewy current; and during
the fifteen days from the mouth of the Ohio to
St. Louis, young Smith learned much of up-stream
travel that was soon to stand him in good stead.

But however arduous the long days might be,
the evenings were a delight. For then, with a
campfire roaring under some spreading tree, the
boatmen would vie with each other in recounting

[1] "Recollections of the Past Ten Years."

the adventures that had befallen them.   Some had
been in the Upper Missouri River country, three
thousand miles away, and had heard the Great
Falls singing thunderously to the empty spaces.
Others had penetrated the forest wilderness above
the Falls of St. Anthony.   Still others had reached
the Spanish country by way of the Red River or
the Arkansas.   One had been to Santa Fé and
" high-walled " Taos, and he remembered weird
tales of deserted prehistoric cities in the mountain fastnesses beyond the Spanish Peaks.   Another had been at the headwaters of the Yellowstone and seen Colter's Hell — a vast patch of
earth where the good God was still at work amidst
primeval fire and steam and brimstone, and as
this man talked, some smiled incredulously, for he
seemed as one who lies blithely for his own amaze-
ment.   And perhaps he did; perhaps they all did
in some degree!

Always at the first peep of day the battle with
the river began again.   They passed the turbulent waters between the Grand Tower and the
Devil's Oven.   The Cornice Rock dropped behind them, and the perilous point called the Syca-
more Root became an unpleasant memory.   Now
they toiled slowly past the mouth of the Kaskaskia, upon which, a few miles inland, stood an important old town of the same name — a pleasant
village, and proud to remember that it had once
entertained the great friend of Liberty, Lafayette.

Now the whitewashed mud walls and the wooden crosses of St. Genevieve were seen on the Missouri side, a mile up the little creek called Gaboureau. To the eastward were the rich alluvial lands of the " American Bottom," and there the scattered farmsteads of the *petits paysans,* or small planters, made the landscape pleasant. More days of gruelling labor, and they saw the shot towers of Herculaneum set high on the bluffs to the west. Past the mouth of the Maramec they forged slowly; past the thriving villages of Carondelet and Cahokia. Then, at last, fifteen days after they had left the mouth of the Ohio, they saw the city of St. Louis rising gradually from the water's edge up the flanks of the westward bluffs; and at a distance it was like a seated throng viewing from a spacious amphitheatre the pageant of the westering peoples!

II

WHEN Jedediah Smith first walked the streets of St. Louis, the town was nearly sixty years old, and its motley population of Spanish, French and Americans numbered somewhat less than five thousand. Though its advantageous position near the central point of a vast system of waterways had made it an important settlement from the time of its founding, yet it had shown little progress until after that day in March, 1804, when, in the course of twenty-four hours, it had flown in succession the flags of Spain, France and the United States in token of the passing sovereignty of the great territory of Louisiana. Shortly thereafter Lewis and Clark had undertaken their famous exploring expedition to the mouth of the Columbia, and the influx of Americans had begun. The Yankee spirit soon transformed the general aspect of the old town. Whereas, before, most of the houses were frame structures daubed with mud and whitewashed, or built of stone in the rough and coated with mortar, brick houses had begun to appear, until

24

in 1819, as a traveller of the time informs us, " lines of buildings containing handsome and spacious city houses " were to be seen —" houses that would not have disgraced Philadelphia." [1] In 1817 the first steamboat, the *Pike,* arrived, and in 1819 the *Independence* made the trip to Franklin and back — the first power boat to sail the Missouri River. During the same year, the *Western Engineer,* bearing the exploring party of Major Long, ascended to a point near the present city of Omaha. But, though the development of steamboat navigation continued steadily from that time on, it was not until the year 1831 that steamboats began to ascend the Missouri as far as the mouth of the Yellowstone, and all traffic on the upper reaches of the Missouri was still by keelboats and mackinaws.

After the transfer of Louisiana to the United States, the fur trade, which had been the chief industry of the town from the beginning, had soon increased in volume as a result of American enterprise. On March 12th, 1811, the Overland Astorians, under the command of W. P. Hunt, had left St. Louis, bound for the mouth of the Columbia, where they expected to join forces with a sea expedition that had left New York harbor on the ship *Tonquin* early in September of the previous year for the long and hazardous voyage around the Horn. The tale of the Astorians, as

[1] Flint. " Recollections," etc.

told by Washington Irving, is one of the master-
pieces of American Literature.

During the war of 1812 the fur trade had declined, and though in the year 1819 five companies
of some importance were operating from St.
Louis, the chief of these being the Missouri Fur
Company, headed by the veteran Spanish trader,
Manuel Lisa, yet none of these was doing a profitable business.

However, Jed had arrived at a most auspicious
time — just when the tide, having reached its lowest ebb, had begun to turn. The great Manuel
Lisa, who had for many years operated on the
Upper Missouri and Yellowstone, had died two
years before and had been succeeded by Joshua
Pilcher as head of the Missouri Fur Company,
which, however, was then nearing the end of its
history. In 1821 Pilcher had established a new
trading post at the mouth of the Bighorn; and
but a few weeks before Smith's arrival, the Company had sent out a party of 180 trappers under
Jones and Immel, bound for the Upper Missouri
country. Though successful at the start, this expedition was doomed to meet disaster at the hands
of the Blackfeet near the Forks of the Missouri,
and its two leaders were never to return.

It is not in keeping with our purpose to follow
here the failing fortunes of the old Missouri Fur
Company, though the bare factual story of that
organization is packed with the precious stuff of

which great epics are made. What does concern our purpose is a brief paragraph that had appeared in the *Missouri Republican* for March 20th, 1822, less than two months before the arrival of our hero. It ran as follows:

TO ENTERPRISING YOUNG MEN

The subscriber wishes to engage one hundred young men to ascend the Missouri River to its source, there to be employed for one, two or three years. For particulars enquire of Major Andrew Henry, near the lead mines in the County of Washington, who will ascend with, and command, the party; or of the subscriber near St. Louis.
(Signed) WILLIAM H. ASHLEY.

The names there given could not but inspire the greatest confidence among the adventurous young spirits of that time and place. Major Henry, born in Fayette County, Pennsylvania, during the early part of the Revolutionary War, had descended the Ohio in his middle twenties. He was one of the incorporators of the Missouri Fur Company in 1809, and in the spring and summer of that year had led an expedition up the Missouri to the Three Forks, where a trading post had been established. Driven thence by the terrible Blackfeet, he had crossed the Continental Divide and built a fort on what has since been called Henry's Fork of the Snake River, thus being the first American trader to operate west of the Rockies. Having spent there the winter of

1810–11, Henry, finding this position also extremely difficult, if not impossible, to hold against the Indians, had returned to St. Louis during the following summer. For ten years now he had been engaged in lead mining, and had come to be known as " Andrew Henry of the Mines "; but the stories of his adventures beyond the Great Divide still passed from mouth to mouth, and we may be sure that they had lost nothing of wonder in the passing.

Though William Henry Ashley had not yet ventured into the wilderness, yet his name had become one to conjure with. Born in Powhatan County, Virginia, in 1778, he had settled in St. Louis in 1802, where he seems very soon to have won prominence. He was made Captain of the Missouri Militia in 1813, Colonel in 1819, and was now General. Two years before, he had been elected Lieutenant Governor of the State, but recently admitted to the Union.

It is not surprising that these illustrious names, together with the new spirit of adventure that was in the air, should have brought a ready response to the advertisement above quoted. Within a fortnight the one hundred young men had been enrolled, " many of whom," as a local paper remarked at the time, " had relinquished the most respectable employments and circles of society " for the dangers and hardships of wilderness life. And what men they were! Fate seems just then to have been in a specially artistic mood, bent upon plotting their story on an epic scale; to this end choosing the most heroic spirits of an heroic region, dooming them to wanderings that should make those of Odysseus and Æneas seem mere pleasure jaunts, preparing amazing adventures for them to encounter, mighty deeds that they should do, and, for many, strange and tragic ends.

On April 15th, 1822, some three weeks before Jed Smith, their future comrade and leader, had set foot upon the St. Louis landing, these hundred men with two keelboats loaded with trapping supplies and goods for the Indian trade, had begun the long ascent of the Missouri under the leadership of Major Henry. General Ashley had accompanied them, intending to ascend to the mouth of the Yellowstone and to return to the States in the fall. The first objective of the expedition was the Three Forks of the Missouri, where, as Rumor had it, " existed a wealth of furs not surpassed by the mines of Peru." From thence trapping parties would work the creeks and rivers on both sides of the Great Divide; and, if circumstances should prove favorable, the party would later move on down the trail of Lewis and Clark even to the mouth of the Columbia.

One can easily imagine what must have been Jed's regret upon hearing everywhere the eager talk about the two great expeditions that had so recently started for the mountains. If he had only come a month earlier, he might even now be far up the river in pursuit of his dream. But perhaps it was just as well after all. With his experience as a clerk on the lake boats of the British fur traders, he found no difficulty in getting employment in an office of one of the St. Louis companies, where he might have the opportunity of becoming familiar with American methods of business. Nor was his great dream idle during the long summer that followed. In any tavern of the town one might meet old Spanish and French veterans of the wilderness, some of whom, no doubt, had been with Lisa at the Three Forks; some with Henry beyond the Rockies; and some must have known the Spanish country and been to Santa Fé. Many were the tales of Indian fights, hairbreadth escapes, and well nigh incredible sufferings from hunger and thirst that these would tell, providing they were first well warmed with the liquor of their liking.

Little by little Jed was able to pick up much of what seemed to be fairly dependable geographical information regarding the Great Northwest and the Great Southwest, all of which he carefully noted on a crude map of the period. But there was a vast triangular space, with its apex somewhere in the Upper Platte region, one leg extending to the Columbia's mouth and the other reaching out toward the Gulf of California, that re-

mained white in spite of his inquiries. Now and
then some old-timer, whose creative faculty had
been somewhat overstimulated, would remember
that he had once met a man whose name he did
not recall, who had heard from someone much
about that interior country. Nevertheless, no information was forthcoming that Jed might record
within that immense blank triangle — the country
of his dream. And so, during the summer of
1822, the dream was nurtured with mystery and
grew mighty.

Nor was Jed the only dreamer in St. Louis.
It was an era of dreaming, for the lure of easy
wealth was in the air and had fastened like an
enchantment upon all men. One had only to get
far enough away from the States to find, in inexhaustible quantities and with all the circumstances
of romance, the means for realizing one's wildest
dream. Somewhere out yonder all the streams
swarmed with beaver, the price of which was rising rapidly. The fur-fever was raging now, just
as the gold-fever would rage a little over a quarter of a century later, and after that the home-
stead-fever. In its issue for September 17th, the
Intelligencer of St. Louis published an article
in which the following paragraph occurred:
"Those formerly engaged in the trade have increased their capital and extended their enter-
prises; many new firms have engaged in it and
others are preparing to do so. It is computed

that a thousand men, chiefly from this place, are now employed on the waters of the Missouri and half that number on the upper Mississippi."

Men were in a mood for hearing big stories that summer and fall. In the absence of reports from the upper country, Rumor worked overtime; and it seemed that nearly every able-bodied man Jed met had set his heart upon " going to the mountains " next year. Then one day during mid-October came what seemed to be unqualified corroboration of the wildest rumors. In the golden autumn doze a fleet of rude mackinaws, under the command of Captain Perkins of the Missouri Fur Company, came drifting down from the mouth of the Missouri, and tied up at the St. Louis landing. They had made the dangerous trip from the upper waters of the far off Yellowstone, and they were laden with costly beaver packs. Twenty-four thousand dollars' worth of fur! The news of their coming had travelled across country from St. Charles on the Missouri, and all St. Louis, it seemed, was crowded along the water front to welcome this Jason and his crew returning with the Golden Fleece. Gaunt with toil and privations, long-haired and bewhiskered, bronzed with the sun and wind of the wilderness, and clad in savage garb, these men were received as conquerors are received. Bells rang in all the steeples, guns roared up and down the river front, dogs barked, men shouted and sang. Far into the night the celebration continued. Bonfires flared. Liquor flowed freely. For this was more than a triumph (alas, the last!) of the old Missouri Fur Company. It was, in a sense, the first, though vicarious, triumph of many a dreamer's dream.

A week later another and smaller party arrived in a mackinaw. It was General Ashley with a handful of men returning from the mouth of the Yellowstone. Once again St. Louis thronged the water front, but the manner of his reception, though hearty enough, no doubt, lacked something of the fervor that the arrival of Captain Perkins had aroused; for Ashley's party came with empty hands, and the story they had to tell must have seemed like an anticlimax. The hundred "enterprising young men," led by Major Henry, had made their way in good time to the mouth of the Yellowstone over two thousand miles away, and there, on the tongue of land between the two rivers, they had begun to build a fort, from whence, as a base, trapping parties might operate. But ill fortune had not been lacking. While still in the State of Missouri, some two days below the mouth of the Kansas River, one of the keelboats, heavily laden with valuable goods, had become unmanageable while crossing the turbulent stream and, drifting against a snag, had been staved and sunk. No lives had been lost, but the cargo, valued at $10,000, had gone to the bottom. Nevertheless, the party had forged ahead without much delay. For weeks thereafter Fate seemed to have been propitiated by that one sacrifice below the Kansas. At the villages of the Ree Indians near the mouth of the Grand River in what is now South Dakota, Major Henry had spent several days in successful trade for horses, and had met no difficulty there, though the Rees had earned a reputation for treachery among the earlier traders. But in the month of August, when the party had passed the Mandan towns, a band of Assiniboines that had, no doubt, been spying upon the Americans for days, had swooped down upon the impotent horse-guards at a time when the main body with the keelboat had crossed with the channel to the opposite shore. Fifty horses, that had but recently been purchased from the Rees, were driven away, while nearly a hundred men, well armed but out of range, gazed across the waste of sand and water and raged to no purpose.

But in spite of these initial disasters, Ashley was not discouraged. With a hundred men already in the fur country, he pointed out that success was only a matter of persistence, and announced his intention of leading a second party up river early in the spring. Among those who enlisted for the great adventure was Jedediah Smith.

III

NORTHBOUND WITH THE ROBINS

IT was on the 10th of March, 1823, that General Ashley started again for the Upper Missouri with a hundred men and two keelboats, *Yellowstone Packet* and *The Rocky Mountains*. And with him went Jedediah Smith in pursuit of a dream grown mighty.

The new grass was like a pale green flame burning slowly up the sloughs, and the young leafage of the cottonwoods was a thin smoke against the sky that day when they started north with the robins. Singing they went, for these hundred men were young with the spirit of adventure, and that is still the youngest thing in the world, though it was already ancient when history began. The rattle of musketry and the shouting along the levee grew dim, and many a youngster, looking back, saw for the last time the smoke of the homefires pluming skyward. Some were to disappear like yonder hearth-reek, leaving no hint of the manner of their passing; and others, bewitched by the wild life and the vast free spaces of the wilderness, would shed, as an uncomfortable coat, the inheritance of ages, lapsing into the primitive,

35

never again to long for the snug comforts and predetermined ways of civilized man.

A day and a night passed, and their boats, swinging westward, had crossed the agitated line that, like a tide rip, marks the thrust of the impetuous Missouri against the slower might of the Mississippi.   At St. Charles farewells were said once more; and then, day by day, signs of civilization became less frequent.   From the mouth of the Kansas, where the western boundary of the States then ran, the spring, still young as at St. Louis, led them north.   Or did their advance progressively awaken the spring?   For weeks, it seemed, the wonder work made no progress.   As it had been at the Kansas, so it was at the Platte and at the Sioux; for the young men and the young sun and the warm southwinds were travelling together.

Though these adventurers were now well beyond the frontiers of civilization, yet it must not be inferred that they were the only white men in that portion of the great Missouri Valley.   Here and there along the river from its mouth to the Three Forks were scattered many trading posts of varying importance.   Above the Kansas they had passed a considerable number of such establishments.   There was one at the Blacksnake Hills, founded by old Joseph Roubidoux near the site of the present St. Joseph.   There was the old trading house of the Choteaus at the mouth of the

Nishnabotna. In the region of the Platte's mouth they had seen the post built during the previous year by Joshua Pilcher of the Missouri Fur Company. Some fifteen miles farther up was old Fort Lisa, then about to be abandoned. Five miles beyond that, near the point where Lewis and Clark held their famous council with the Otoe and Missouri Indians, stood Fort Atkinson, then the northermost military post of the United States on the Missouri River. It was commanded at that time by Colonel Leavenworth who was soon to win doubtful laurels as leader of the "Missouri Legion" in the Ree Campaign. There were American traders at Blackbird Hill near the old mud village of the Omaha Indians; and at the mouth of the Big Sioux, where Sioux City now stands, the American Fur Company maintained a house. At most of these points Ashley's men had rested long enough to exchange gossip fresh from the States for news from the great upper country.

On into the North they forged with pole and oar and sail and cordelle; but now it was May, and the pale green spring somehow began to outpace them at last, though they could not say just when they had dropped behind. The grass in the sloughs seemed suddenly to have deepened and darkened, and the full-leafed cottonwoods were ready for the heavy heat of the summer, as yet withheld. Past the mouth of the Vermillion

they toiled; past the Rivière à Jacques; past Ponca
Post where the fleet Niobrara assails the Missouri
with a roar and hurls it back despite its greater
mass.   They were now in the country of the powerful Sioux tribe, which, though destined to make
the last great stand of all the prairie peoples
against the westering Aryan forty years later, was
still friendly to the whites.

Hitherto, the northward march of Ashley's
party had seemed little more than a pleasure
jaunt, for though the labor at the cordelle was no
child's play, it was divided among a hundred
men, and no unforeseen obstacles had been encountered.   But soon they were to hear that
which should put a new face upon the whole adventure, shatter the illusions of the attenuated
pussy-willow spring.   At noon one day they toiled
past the White River coming in on their left;
and when the sun was level with the bluffs, they
swung around a right hand bend, and paused to
shout.   There, a little way ahead of them, was
American Island, green with cedars, and at its
lower point stood Fort Recovery, the Sioux trading post of the Missouri Fur Company — a cluster of log cabins surrounded by a wall of sharp-
ened pickets.

Many of Ashley's party and the men at the fort
had known each other since boyhood, and it is
easy to imagine how the evening was spent.   But
the news that the newcomers received in return

for the latest gossip from home was hardly re-
assuring. The Rees, it appeared, were in a bad
mood. Two months before, a band of over a
hundred had boldly entered the Sioux country,
robbed a party of white traders and, encouraged
by this initial success, had attacked the fort. In
the brisk battle that followed, several of the Indians had been wounded and two had been killed,
one of the latter being the son of a chief. Since
that time, persistent rumors had been coming
down stream to the effect that the tribe intended
to leave its villages near the mouth of the Grand,
join forces with the Mandans near the mouth of
the Knife, and resist any attempt on the part of
the traders to pass that point.

The assembled parties at Fort Recovery could
not know that this apparently unwarranted
flare-up of the Rees was not merely a matter of
whim on the part of that particular people. It
was, in fact, symptomatic of a widespread spirit
of opposition among the tribes of a vast region,
due to the large number of traders that were entering the country with the revival of the fur
trade. It could not be known that, far away at
the Three Forks, Jones and Immel, who had gone
out with one hundred eighty men during the
previous spring, were even then approaching death
and disaster at the hands of the Blackfeet; and
that bad news was already on the way from Henry
on the upper river.

But even considering the affair solely as a matter of Ree caprice, and assuming that the Mandans had no notion of joining forces with their neighbors to the south, Ashley was confronted with a dilemma.   The Ree villages were strongly fortified and commanded the river.   It appeared that a wedge was about to be driven between the ascending party and Henry at the Yellowstone's mouth; for the overland trip was, of course, impossible without many pack horses, and only among the Rees themselves, it was thought, could a number sufficient for such an undertaking be found.   The only course possible was to run the gauntlet of the Indian villages with the boats. After all, the mood of the Rees might have changed by now; and there was much in the history of the tribe to justify such a hope, for no trader ever knew which way the wind of their whim might blow.

Accordingly, the early dawn saw Ashley's hundred moving northward again.   Four days passed by without any noteworthy incident; and then at noon of the fifth day, when they were nearing the mouth of the Cheyenne, an express arrived with news from their comrades in the upper country. Things had not been going well with Major Henry.   Having left his new post in charge of a small band, he had pushed on up the Missouri early in the spring.   Near the Great Falls he had encountered a hostile party of Blackfeet.   De-

feated and forced to retreat, he was now waiting
for reinforcements at the mouth of the Yellowstone. He had lost most of his horses, and asked
that at least fifty should be purchased by Ashley
from the Rees, for none could be procured in his
vicinity. He inclined to the opinion that the
treachery of the Assiniboines during the previous
fall and the recent resistance of the Blackfeet
might be traced to the influence of the British
traders who naturally looked with disfavor upon
the advance of American trappers toward the
rich fur country of the Columbia and its tributaries.

Plainly enough, the key to success for both parties was held by the Rees! They had the needed
horses and they held the river.

Clinging to the hope that all might still be
well, Ashley pushed on up stream. At sunset on
the 29th of May the party camped at the mouth
of the Grand some five or six miles below the
Ree towns. In mid-afternoon of the next day
they rounded a bend where the river, flowing for
some distance from east to west, turns abruptly
south, and saw along the north bank, not more
than half a mile ahead, a clutter of mud lodges
and a portion of a newly built stockade that apparently surrounded the settlement.

The cordelle crews were now taken aboard,
rifles were placed in easy reach of the men, and
the boats, proceeding with oars and poles to a

point in front of the lower village, were anchored
in mid-stream.   The two towns, set upon the flat
lands in two convex bends that joined at the mouth
of a little creek flowing from the north, were
now visible to the men on the keelboats; and each
of the one hundred forty-one lodges was like a
hornet's nest boiling forth its swarm.   The gut-
tural voices of men, the high pitched, querulous
cries of the squaws, and the barking of the dogs
ran over the settlement.   Many a youth who was
making his first trip into the wilds thought wist-
fully of home in those tense moments, wondering
why he had ever wished to leave.

A Canadian boatman, who had been with Henry
west of the Rockies, mounted the low roof of the
Yellowstone's cabin, cupped his hands about his
mouth and shouted a greeting to the Rees.   The
hubbub among the nearby lodges subsided as he
began to talk in the universal sign language of the
plains, indicating the peaceful nature of the white
men's mission and their wish to enter into a parley.   The reply from the Rees seemed friendly;
and, seeing three Indians, two of whom were evidently chiefs, making their way toward the river
bank, General Ashley, with two men, put off in
a skiff and met them on the strip of sandy beach.

Now it happened, whether by good fortune or
ill remained yet to be seen, that the man who accompanied the two chiefs to the parley was the
notorious Edward Rose, the sound of whose name,

mentioned at intervals from the Gulf of Mexico to
the Three Forks of the Missouri, would at that
time have awakened in sequence every note in the
gamut of emotion from contempt or fear to ad-
miration. The son of a white trader and a half-
breed negro and Cherokee woman, Rose had
achieved notoriety during the closing years of the
18th century as one of a band of pirates operating
among the islands of the lower Mississippi.
About the year 1807, the business of piracy seems
to have become too hazardous even for a man of
Rose's nature, and he had fled to the wild country
where a man might still be free to exercise his
more robust talents.   Within a year or two thereafter, thanks to shrewdness, audacity, undeniable
courage, and a dusky skin, he had arisen to a position of great power among the Crow Indians,
whose country lay south of the Yellowstone and
west of the Powder River.   In 1811 he was
among the Rees when the Overland Astorians under W. P. Hunt passed that way, and he had
acted as a guide for the westbound party from
the Missouri to the Country of the Crows, with
whom he remained until about 1820, when he had
taken up his abode among the Rees.

Recognizing the man at once by the disfiguring
scar of an old cutlass wound across the nose, by
reason of which he was generally known as *Nez
Coupé*, Ashley greeted him warmly; for the success of the present venture might easily depend

upon the influence of this ex-pirate. For a suitable consideration Rose agreed to act as interpreter. The two parties squatted in a circle on the sand, and the pipe was passed in dignified silence, while the boat-crews in mid-stream and the Indians, crowded on the roofs of their mud lodges, looked on in a hush of expectancy. When the preliminary ceremony was over, the General opened the parley. His heart was good and he would speak straight words to his brothers, the Rees. The white men at the fort on the Island of the Cedars in the country of the Sioux had told him things that were not good to hear. He was sad when he heard that there had been trouble between the Rees and the white men down yonder; and he had grieved to hear that a chief's son had been killed. All the way up from the Island of the Cedars he had been thinking hard about this thing; and he had feared that the Rees might feel angry at all white men because of what had happened. That would be wrong. It was not, however, a weak heart that made him speak so. His heart was very strong, for he was a big chief in his own country; and had he not a hundred brave men out yonder on the boats? And each of them had grown up with a rifle and could shoot straight. He knew that if there should be trouble, many Rees would surely die. And that was not good to think about. He had passed that

way a year ago and had stopped to trade with the
Rees.   They had been very kind, and so his heart
was warm toward them.   His friends, who were
at the mouth of the Yellowstone, needed more
horses which were not to be had up there, because
the Assiniboines were not rich as the Rees were.
He wished to buy horses and go on to his friends.
He had spoken.

At the conclusion of the General's speech, the
chiefs withdrew for a private conference; and
when they returned, after what had seemed an
interminable period to the anxious white men,
they brought soft words.   They too had been
sad to hear of what had happened at the Island
of the Cedars; but three moons had grown old
and died since then, and they no longer remembered.   As the black trail of a prairie fire is made
green with rain, so their hearts were green again.
Those were all young men who had gone down
yonder, wishing to be brave and being only foolish.
Young men were like that, and would not listen
to the old men whom many winters had made wise.
They knew the big white chief before them spoke
straight words.   Also, their own tongues were
not forkéd.   They had many good horses — so
many that one could not see them all with a look.
They would trade.   The Ree chiefs had spoken.

Ashley now gave liberal gifts of scarlet cloth
to the chiefs and, having agreed upon the mer-

chandise that should be exchanged for the horses
(which included a liberal supply of powder and
ball), the white men returned to the boats. The
tense silence that had clung about the party in
mid-stream during the parley, now gave way to
singing and laughter and jest, as the men made
ready for the trade. Raw youths, out of sheer
relief from dread, boasted valiantly. If the Rees
wanted trouble, they knew very well where they
could get it in plenty! Here, evidently, was a
good example of crossing bridges before you
reached them. In a few weeks now the two
parties would be united on the Yellowstone, and
where was the parcel of niggers that could stop
two hundred white men? However, some of the
older members of the party examined their rifle-
locks, and were silent.

Shortly after noon the dickering began. It
continued until sunset; and all next day they hag-
gled, Yankee shrewdness and Indian cunning con-
testing every point as the shaggy ponies came up
for appraisal. By evening of the first of June
the desired number of animals had been purchased,
and, uneasy with their hobbles, these milled and
nickered on the beach. During the bartering arrangements had been made for a party to set out
with the herd at dawn for the cross-country trip
to the mouth of the Yellowstone. Forty of the
more dependable men were chosen for this task,
and among the number was Jedediah Smith.

As twilight deepened, the overland party made a semi-circular camp which, with the river, enclosed the herd; and a crescent of driftwood fires was glowing when the dark came down.

IV

THE BATTLE

THE camp fires on the beach burned low, serving only to heighten the sense of companionship among the men; for it was a sultry night. Sounds carried far. A dog-feast was being held somewhere in the upper village, and now and then the drums of the dance boomed through the soft dusk that was odorous with the young summer. At times, the bass voices of the singing braves roared above the drums, and out of these soared the thin-spun notes of the squaws. Then the song would cease abruptly, and in the succeeding hush the droning of insect life and the mumble of the river would come back — like the sense of dear and common things. Sometimes a *voyageur* on the black boats would fling a snatch of song across the forty yards of darkling water that separated the parties, and the camp on shore would catch it up boisterously, and set the horses neighing. Or some wag in the camp, remembering a current jest at the expense of a comrade out yonder, would hurl it at the boats, receiving a good-natured verbal drubbing for his pains, till the distant bluffs joined in the laughter.

It was the time when men remember tales, and about those fires where yarns were being spun, the groups increased.

" Go ahead and roll us out some of your doin's that time across the plains," said a youngster, lounging in one of the larger groups, to an old-timer who had been to Santa Fé and had scars to show.   " You seed sights that spree, eh? " [1]

" Well, we did! " the old timer replied.

Far off thunder mumbled as the party waited for the yarning to begin.

" Some of 'em got their flints fixed this side of Pawnee Fork," so the old veteran began at length, " and a heap of mule meat went wolfing.   Just by Little Arkansaw we saw the first Injun.   Me and young Somes was ahead for meat, and I had hobbled the old mule and was approachin' some goats, when I see the critturs turn back their heads and jump right away from me.   ' Hurraw, Dick! ' I shouts, ' hyar's brown skin a comin'! '   And off I makes for my mule.   The young greenhorn sees the goats runnin' up to him, and not being up to Injun ways, he blazes at the first and knocks him over.   Jest then seven red heads tops the bluff, and seven Pawnees come a-screechin' on us.   I cuts the hobbles and jumps on the mule, and when I looks back, there was Dick Somes rammin' a ball down his gun like mad, and the Injuns

[1] The two tales in this chapter are borrowed, with slight changes, from Ruxton's " Life in the Far West," as being typical of the campfire yarns of the period.

flingin' their arrows at him pretty smart, I tell you. 'Hurraw, Dick, mind your hair!' And I ups old Greaser and let one Injun have it as was goin' plum through the boy with his lance. *He* turned on his back handsome, and Dick gets the ball down at last, blazes away and drops another. Then we charged on 'em, and they clears off like runnin' cows. I takes the hair off the heads of the two as we made meat of; and I do believe thar's some of them scalps on my leggin's yet.

"Well, Dick was as full of arrows as a porky-pine; one was stickin' right through his cheek, one in his meat-bag, and two more 'bout his hump-ribs. I tuk 'em all out slick, and away we goes to camp, and carryin' the goat too. 'Injuns! Injuns!' was what the greenhorns yelled; 'we'll be tackled tonight, that's sartin!' 'Tackled be damned!' says I; 'ain't we men too, and white at that?'

"Well, as soon as the animals was unpacked, the guvner sends out a strong guard, seven boys, and old hands at that. It was pretty nigh on sundown. The boys was drivin' in the animals, when, *howgh-owgh-owgh-owgh* we hears right behind the bluffs; and 'bout a minute and a crowd of Injuns gallops down on the animals. Wagh! Warn't thar hoopin'! We jumps for the guns, but before we got to the fires, the Injuns was among the herd. I saw Ned Collyer and his brother, who was in the hoss-guard, let drive at

'em; but twenty Pawnees was round 'em before
the smoke cleared from their guns; and when the
crowd broke, the two boys was on the ground and
their hair gone. Thar war an Englishman that
just saved the herd. He had his mare, a reg'lar
buffler-runner, picketed right handy, and as soon
as he sees the fix, he jumps on her and rides right
into the thick of the mules, and passes through
'em firin' his two-shot gun at the Injuns; and by
gor he made two come. The mules, which was
snortin' with funk and runnin' before the Injuns,
as soon as they see the Englishman's mare, followed her right back into the corral, and thar
they was safe. Fifty Pawnees came screechin'
after 'em, but we was ready that time, and the
way we throwed 'em was something handsome.
But three of the hoss-guards got skeered — least-
wise their mules did, and carried 'em off into the
perairy, and the Injuns dashed after 'em. Them
pore devils looked back, miserable now, I tell ye,
with about a hundred red varmints tearin' after
their hair, and hoopin' like mad. Young Jem
Belcher was the last; and when he seed it was no
use, and his time was nigh, he throwed himself
off his mule, and standin' as straight as a hickory
wipin' stick, he waves his hand to us, and blazes
away at the first Injun as come up, and drops him
slick; but the next moment, you may guess, *he*
died. We couldn't do nothin', for before our
guns was loaded, all three was dead and their hair

was gone.   Five of our boys got rubbed out that time, and seven Injuns lay wolf's meat, while a many more went off gut-shot, I'll lay!   Howsoever, five of us went under, and the Pawnees made a raise of a dozen mules.   Wagh!"

A low, incessant rumbling, punctuated by an occasional earth-shaking bump far off in the dark Northwest now overlaid and dimmed the droning of the bugs.   Coyotes yammered from the bluffs, and now and then Ree dogs answered, howling.

"I'll say as how we are in for a right smart storm of rain and thunder," remarked old Glass, arising and peering in the direction from whence a faint breath of wind had sprung out of a rising wall of murk that was slowly blotting out the stars.   But the old-timer was in a mood for more yarning.   "Yes, sir!" he was saying.   "I went out that time old Jim lost his animals.   A hundred and forty mules froze that night, wagh!   Old Bill Laforey was thar; and the cussedest liar was Bill — for lies tumbled out of his mouth like boudins out of a buffler's stomach.   He was the child as saw the putrefied forest!   I mind when Bill come in to St. Louis once; and one day he was fixed up like a dandy and a-settin' in the tavern when a lady says to him: 'Well, Mister Laforey,' she says; 'I hear as how you're a great trav'ler.'

"'Trav'ler, marm,' says Bill; 'this nigger's

no trav'ler. I are a trapper, marm, a mountain-man, wagh!'

" ' Well, Mister Laforey,' says the lady, ' trap-pers is great trav'lers, and you goes over a sight of ground in your perishinations, I'll be bound to say!'

" ' A sight, marm, this coon's gone over,' says Bill, ' if that's the way your stick floats. I've trapped beaver on Arkansaw and away up on Yallerstone. I've fout the Blackfeet; I've raised the hair of more'n one Apach', and made a 'Rapaho come afore now. And scalp my old head, marm, but I've seed a putrefied forest,' says Bill.

" ' La, Mister Laforey — a what?' says the lady.

" ' A putrefied forest, marm,' says Bill, ' as sure as my rifle's got hind sights! One day we crossed a canyon and over a divide and got into a perairy whar was green grass, and green trees, and green leaves on the trees, and birds singin' in the green leaves, and this in Febr'ary, wagh! Our animals was like to die when they see the green grass, and we all sung out, Hurraw for summer doin's! And I jest ups old Ginger at one of them singin' birds, and down come the crittur elegant, its head spinnin' away from the body, but never stops singin'. I finds it was stone, wagh! And old Rube, what was with us, ups with his ax and lets drive at a cottonwood. *Schruk-k-k!* goes the ax agin the tree, and out comes a bit of the blade as big as my hand. We looks at the animals, and thar they stood shakin' over the grass, which I'm dog-gone if it warn't stone too. And a feller as knowed everything came up and he scrapes the trees with his butcher knife, and snaps the grass like pipe stems, and breaks the leaves like shells. He said it was putrefactions!'

" ' La, Mister Laforey,' says the lady; ' did the leaves and grass smell bad?'

" ' Smell bad, marm?' says Bill; ' would a polecat as was froze to stone smell bad? If it warn't a putrefied perairy, marm, then this hoss don't know fat cow from poor bull, nohow!'

" Well," resumed the old-timer, when the roar of laughter had subsided, " Old Bill Laforey is gone under now. Went trappin' with a Frenchman who shot him for his bacca and traps. And that reminds me. Has any of you'ns got any bacca? This beaver feels like chawin'."

A sudden gust of cool wind sent the embers scurrying and made the tent poles creak. The drums in the upper village no longer boomed, and the singing voices were stilled. Even the coyotes had ceased to cry. But as the men peered to windward into the murk where sheet lightning leaped fitfully, they heard but a little way up the valley the roaring of wind-embattled trees and the many-footed tumult of the charging rain.

Scarcely had the tent-pins been secured to windward and the horse guards taken their allotted stations about the excited herd, when the storm broke. For hours it raged, and whoever peeped through a tent flap into the leaping flare of the lightning, saw the world as a freshly painted monotone smeared and blurred by the sweep of some huge brush dipped in electric blue.

Lulled by the monotonous uproar of the storm, the camp slept at last, unconscious of a sinister activity in the villages. Shortly before the tempest struck, Edward Rose, who had been mingling with the dancers at the dog-feast in the upper town, had stolen away from the revellers and, putting off in a canoe, paddled out to the keelboat *Yellowstone*. Taking Ashley aside, he had expressed doubts as to the good intentions of the Rees. What made him doubt? No more than a feeling he had that something was going wrong. Ashley, doubting Rose more than the Rees, had gone to bed little troubled.

About midnight the fury of the storm ceased, but the heavy downpour continued through the pitch-black hours. At half past three a dripping horse-guard, with bad news to tell, awoke General Ashley. Aaron Stephens had been killed in the upper village, and it seemed probable that the Rees might begin an attack on the boats and the camp at any moment. The General sent the guard back to arouse the men on shore, and soon both parties with their rifles in readiness, were peering anxiously into the black drench; and the dread was the greater in that nothing was visible. Time seemed to have grown sluggish with the rain chill and the drowse of the wee hours. It was the time when courage is at its lowest ebb, and the unresolved sighing of the rain was like a doleful prophecy to many a youth who now for the first time looked forward to battle. Slowly the minutes crawled dawnward. The droning of the rain lessened like the sound of a huge revolving wheel losing speed. By and by the blackness began to dissolve into melancholy drab, and the lodges of the Ree loomed ominously in the drizzle.

Tediously the fading of the dark went on. The line of pickets surrounding the village was now visible. Nothing seemed to be moving there. Would anything happen after all? A sense of relief spread through the camp on shore. The men ventured to talk now, for the rain had ceased, and the familiar world was coming back with the slow light. Peacefully the dusky boats swung at anchor in mid-stream. The horses stood quietly, huddled together with drooping necks and steaming hides. Soon the clouds would break, the sun would rise, the westward journey would begin, and laughter would be the end of the night's anxiety.

The crack of a rifle and a spurt of smoke from a

central point in the line of pickets brought the men
to their feet.   A horse screamed and floundered
in the sand, and the herd whinnied and milled.
Then suddenly the whole length of the Indian
stockade roared into smoke, and simultaneously
the wet beach spurted jets of sand.   More horses
went down screaming, and the hobbled herd
plunged and jostled helplessly.

Ben Sneed, Tully Piper and Reed Gibson were
down, the latter struggling to get up, the two
others lying very still.   General Ashley's lack of
judgment in placing the horses and the overland
party on the beach was now painfully apparent;
for no way of retreat was open except toward
the river.   In the disorder that followed the first
sweeping volley of the Rees, it was, curiously
enough, not one of the old-timers who strove to
draw the panicky men into some plan of action,
but one of the youngest of the band, one who had
never before heard the snarl of hostile bullets —
Jedediah Smith.   With the quiet courage and
practical good sense that were to characterize his
short but brilliant career, Jed turned his attention
to the horses.   He saw that the enemy was bent
upon wiping out the herd, and even in the excitement of the attack he realized to the full the
meaning of such a loss, both to the embattled
party and to Henry far away on the Yellowstone.
Calling John Matthews, John Collins, and Jim
Daniels to aid him, he coolly set about the task

of cutting the hobbles of the horses, intent upon driving them into the stream and forcing them to swim across to safety.

By this time the attack had settled down to a brisk running fire up and down the whole line of pickets and from the adjoining shelter of tumbled sand banks. The Rees were armed with London fusils, furnished by British traders from the North, and it was Ashley's own powder and lead that now worked havoc with his plans. A great portion of the firing was being concentrated upon the animals, and many were going down. Some, feeling themselves free of the hobbles, raced neighing down the beach until a raking volley rolled them. Some few ran the gauntlet of the pickets unhurt, and disappeared in the brush. When the three men whom he had summoned to his aid had been shot down, Smith gave up the attempt and joined in the battle.

Joe Gardner was dead, and David Howard and George Flagler would never see St. Louis again. Anger at the sight of their comrades falling about them had served to steady the band, and all now were fighting like veterans. Thilless, the black man, with a bullet hole through both legs, was busy loading and firing from a sitting position, cheerily announcing to his comrades now and then: " They ain't killed this niggah yet! " Old Hugh Glass, bleeding from a hip-wound, was plying the warrior's trade in a cool, methodical manner, always watching for an Indian's head to appear above the pickets or the patch of broken ground before he pressed the trigger. In much the same leisurely manner, the old-timer, who had survived many a scrimmage, went about the business of killing, now and then giving vent to his satisfaction with an Arapahoe war-whoop.

It was a gallant standup fight, but it was hopeless from the first. Even when Ashley managed to put the skiffs ashore in spite of the shower of bullets that whipped the river, only seven of the party on the beach — two of those being seriously wounded — were willing to accept this means of escape. They had seen their comrades slain and their horses slaughtered. Their blood was up — and it was the blood of Kentuckians and Virginians and Pennsylvanians. Many of them were for storming the villages, if only the party on the boats would come and help. But the party on the boats, composed largely of French *voyageurs,* had already mutinied at Ashley's command to move inshore. Only with great difficulty had the General been able to induce a handful of the more courageous to land with the skiffs. Shortly after the skiffs had pulled away, the shore party saw the keelboats dropping down stream and out of the fight. Deserted by their comrades, with half their number either dead or wounded, they realized at last the folly of further resistance. Leaping into the river, they struck out after the boats.

Some, miscalculating the strength of the current, were swept away and lost. Some of the wounded went down and were seen no more. Several were shot as they swam, and disappeared.

It had been a struggle of magnificent courage against an alliance of treachery and cowardice; and the latter had won. Many of the youngsters, who had never fought before, were sobbing with rage and shame as, drenched and bleeding, they were dragged aboard by their faithless comrades.

V

THE EXPRESS TO HENRY

I N a letter written two days after the battle to Major O'Fallon, Indian Agent at Fort Atkinson, Ashley has set down for posterity the story of his woes.[1] " I ordered the boats landed at the first timber for the purpose of putting the men and boats in a better situation to pass the villages in safety," so the letter continues after giving an account of the catastrophe. " When my intentions were made known, to my surprise and mortification, I was told by the men (with but few exceptions) that under no circumstances would they make a second attempt to pass without a large reinforcement. Finding that no arguments that I could use would cause them to change their resolution, I commenced making arrangements for the security of my property. The men proposed that if I would descend the river to this place (near the mouth of the Moreau River), fortify the boats, or make any other defense for their security, they would remain with me until I could receive aid from Major Henry, or from some other quarter. I was compelled to agree to the proposition. On my arrival here, I found them as

much determined to go lower. A resolution has
been formed by the most of them to desert. I
called for volunteers to remain with me under any
circumstances until I should receive the expected
aid. Thirty only volunteered. Among them
were few boatmen, consequently I am compelled
to send one boat back. After taking a part of
her cargo on board this boat (*Yellowstone
Packet*), the balance will be stored at the first
fort below." The rest of the letter is concerned
with the hope that government forces may be
sent " to make these people (the Rees) account
for the outrage committed."

We may imagine that it was a sullen and crestfallen party that landed " at the first timber "
below the scene of disaster; and that nearly all refused to make an immediate attempt to pass the
Ree towns is not strange. Those who had fought
on shore had seen just how far their comrades
could be trusted for support; and though Ashley's courage could not be questioned, his conspicuous lack of generalship was scarcely calculated to fill his men with confidence.

While the boats were lying ashore at the first
timber, a funeral service was held on board the
keelboat *Yellowstone* for one John Gardner, who
died of wounds shortly after the battle. We have
old Hugh Glass's word for it, in a quaint letter
dispatched by him to the dead boy's relatives, that
" **Mr. Smith**, a young man of our company, made

a powerful prayr wh moved us all greatly, and I am persuaded John died in peace." [1]

When the party refused to brave the Rees again, Ashley decided to summon Major Henry to his aid. But the distance to the mouth of the Yellowstone was close upon two hundred miles as the crow flies; and considering the warlike mood of the Indian tribes at that time, the journey would be extremely hazardous. Who, in the present mood of defeat that had settled upon the party, would venture upon such a mission? Lining up his men, Ashley stated the case and made an appeal for volunteers. Only one man stepped out of the line. It was Jedediah Smith. Many wondered at this, and especially the old-timers. A young man who prayed like a parson and was more daring than the tough old mountain men! According to their experience, it didn't appear reasonable; and yet it was so!

Notwithstanding Jed's expressed willingness to set forth without human companionship, Ashley insisted that the young man should not go alone, and finally succeeded in inducing one Baptiste, a French-Canadian trapper, to undertake the journey. Several of the horses that had managed to escape unwounded were found grazing in the timber that fringed the river; and these having been caught with little difficulty, preparations were made for the perilous cross-country ride.

[1] "South Dakota Historical Collections." Vol. I.

When the dark had fallen, the two men, each armed with a rifle, a pistol, and a hunting knife, mounted and rode westward out of the wood. Crossing the bottom and ascending a low range of bluffs, they saw behind them the broad glooming valley, mysterious under the stars, and the glimmering strip that was the river. Far away in front, where the sky still held a pale reminder of the way the sun had gone, the prairie was a billowing dusk, the higher ridges looming vaguely in the wash of the starshine — vast distances, rather felt than seen.

Spurring their tough little horses into a jog trot, and keeping the North Star above their right shoulders, Jed and the Frenchman forged on into an unknown land, heading for the Yellowstone that was somewhere out yonder beyond the rim of the night. Wolves howled occasionally from the hill tops and the prairie owls raised their voices in the joyless, unearthly laughter that they know Slowly the hours dragged on, and the men, riding silently knee to knee, had little sense of progress save when creek or coulee had to be crossed. The Dipper, which is the time-piece of the heavens, seemed at times to have stuck on the upward swing about the Pole; yet suddenly it was up, and after that the increasing drowsiness, against which the riders struggled, gave speed to the starry clock. Thrice the Frenchman nodded, and thrice the swinging dipper leaped ahead for him. Nod-

ding again, he raised his face to the sky and saw
that the gloom was fading out in the vast hollow.
Far across the rolling prairie to the rear a faint
streak of light was visible. The stars were burning low, and the landscape was beginning to lift
out of the dusk. To their right, about a mile distant, a strip of timber marked the course of the
Grand River, and riding thither they descended
into the valley and camped near the water where
a patch of lush grass grew. Here, while the
weary horses, tied to convenient bullberry bushes,
fed contentedly, Jed and Baptiste ate a scanty
breakfast and lay down to rest.

The reaction from the tense experience of the
previous morning, together with the fatigue of the
long night ride, soon sent them into a sound sleep.
After what seemed no more than a few minutes,
Jed, startled by a shrill neighing, leaped up, ex-
pecting to see the long line of pickets spouting
smoke and a kicking tangle of wounded horses on
the beach. Baptiste was also up, clutching his
rifle and blinking at the peaceful valley in momentary bewilderment. In the mind of one rudely
awakened from deep sleep, much may happen in
the first wild instants of returning consciousness.
Glancing at the stream, Jed marvelled to see it
flowing backwards! In the morning it should be
flowing *toward* the sun, and now it was most certainly flowing *away* from the morning that was
no more than a half hour old. Then he knew that

they had slept all day and that the sun was near to setting.   Again the horses neighed, pricking their ears and gazing down stream with heads held high and tails up.   A faint answer, as of many horses whinnying together, came back.

Jed and Baptiste, now broad awake, saw a band of mounted Indian warriors filing diagonally down the flank of the bluff into the valley no more than half a mile to the east.   There seemed to be at least twenty-five in the band, and it was plain now that the white men had been discovered, for after a moment of agitation, the party separated, some dashing on down into the valley and out of sight among the trees, others hurrying back to the open prairie from whence they had just come.

Fortunately, Jed and Baptiste had not unsaddled.   They had intended to rest only long enough for the horses to feed, wishing to put as much space as possible between them and the Rees before they ventured on a good sound sleep.   In a few moments they had mounted and were plunging down the valley in and out among the plum thickets and the bullberry clumps.   Now a steep bluff, closing in to the water's edge, forced them to ford the stream; now for a few hundred yards they found good footing and made the most of it; now again they were crashing through brush into another open space.   They knew that the chances favored them, for their own horses were fresh after a long day of grazing, and doubtless their pursuers had been riding since daybreak. If they were able to gain only slightly during the few remaining hours of light, their chances for escaping in the dark would be good.

The sun set, the twilight deepened, the stars came out. Reining their lathered and winded horses to a stand, they listened and heard only the sighing of a light breeze from the west. Nevertheless, if the Indians had persisted in the pursuit, which seemed likely, they could not be more than three or four miles behind. To ascend the sloping bluffs to the right and take the open prairie might bring the white men into contact with the party that had turned back to the highland. The bluffs to the left were precipitous, and to seek for a way out in that direction would involve much loss of time. Riding on down the valley at a walk, the two men were discussing the situation when Baptiste abruptly checked his horse and sniffed the air.

"*Nom de Dieu!*" he whispered; "it ees smoke! Rees, maybe. What we do now?"

Jed had also caught the smell of smouldering wood. "Stay here with the horses," said he, "and wait till I come back." Pushing cautiously through a wild-cherry thicket and rounding the base of a bluff that jutted into the valley, he saw, about a hundred yards ahead, the black mass of a cluster of cottonwoods splashed with the glow of a dying fire. The light appeared to come from

one point; and if this were true, the party camping
there was probably small, for the great storm had
brought a cold wave and the night air was uncom-
fortably chill.

Jed began to crawl toward the glow, feeling
ahead of him as he went and carefully removing
any sticks that lay in his path, lest the snapping of
one might arouse those about the fire. By and
by, peering through a screen of brush, he saw the
camp. At first glance, there seemed to be only
one man — unmistakably a Ree. He was sitting
cross-legged before a small heap of glowing embers, and he was evidently very sleepy, for his chin
rested on his breast. But when Jed's eyes became
adjusted to the glow, he saw that the man was not
alone. Two other warriors, apparently sound
asleep, lay sprawled upon the grass with their feet
to the fire, their bodies looming dim in the shadows. Three black bulks — horses, by the sound
of nipping and blowing that came from them —
were barely visible in the deeper gloom of the cottonwoods.

"The villages are probably short of meat,"
thought Jed, "and this is a scouting party that
has been looking for buffalo and is now waiting for the main body of hunters."

Jed crawled back to the waiting Frenchman and
reported what he had seen. "It's the safest way
out, Baptiste," he said. "Our horses are a bit
weary, and the Rees owe us many."

" Scalps too ! " whispered the Frenchman, evidently gloating over the prospect for avenging the death of his comrades in the battle on the beach.

Having agreed upon the plan of attack, they tied their horses and started, walking until they had rounded the jutting bluff. Here they cocked their rifles and began to crawl, Jed leading and carefully clearing the way as before. Soon they were peering through the brush within twenty yards of the camp. The man by the fire had not moved.

" Ready," whispered Jed. At the roar of his gun, the man who had been sitting, leaped up with a wild yell, staggered, and fell across the embers. Simultaneously the two shadowy sleepers scrambled to their feet, and at the sound of Baptiste's rifle, one went down. The other had seized his gun, but with a warwhoop from the Frenchman the white men broke from cover with drawn pistols.

" Examine the horses, Baptiste," said Jed when the brief affair was over; " and choose the two best, while I fetch ours."

When, after a few minutes, Jed emerged from the dark, leading the fagged animals, he found the Frenchman wiping three dripping scalps on the grass.

" It's bad enough to be forced to kill," said Smith, " but this is a heathen practice ! "

" *Enfant de Gârce!* " exclaimed Baptiste, whose

experience among the wild tribes of the North had developed the latent savagery that is in most men; "*c'est la guerre! Moi, je suis* mountain man! By and by you mountain man too; then — wagh!" He finished with a sweep of his reeking knife about his left fist by way of indicating the warrior's rite of "lifting hair"; and with a chuckle of satisfaction tucked the hideous souvenirs under his belt and wiped his hands on his buckskin trousers.

Hurriedly now they shifted their saddles to the taller and rangier horses of their fallen foes, leaving the third horse tied as they had found him; and half the night, as they pushed rapidly westward, they heard their own discarded animals, weary with the recent flight, neighing and floundering through the brush in the rear. Then the sounds ceased. When day broke, the riders ventured to ascend the bluffs by way of a winding gully, and halting on a summit that commanded a view of the river and prairie for many miles, they saw no living thing but a wolf loping along a distant ridge and a flock of crows hunting for a feast.

They camped in a bullberry thicket, staked their horses out to graze, and spent the day resting, each taking his turn on guard while the other slept. When the valley began to fill with blue shadows, they set out again, following the stream. It was not yet midnight by the Dipper when they reached the place where the river forks; and being uncer tain as to which branch would be the better, they struck out across the open prairie on what they judged to be the shortest route to the Yellowstone.

Guided by the North Star, they made good progress for several hours, when the sky became overcast. Still they pushed on, trusting to luck and to the sense of direction they still felt. But steadily the night grew blacker, and by and by a drizzling rain began to fall. It soon increased to a sodden, passionless downpour. Suddenly Jed became aware that, so far as he was concerned, there were but three directions — out and up and down!

"No use going on, Baptiste," he said; "for we might find ourselves back at the forks in the morning."

They staked their horses, and, sitting huddled together with their blankets over their heads, waited for the morning. It came at last — an ooze of drab light through the drifting rain. With heads and tails drooping and dripping, feet drawn together, the chilled horses presented a spectacle of misery. The emerging landscape would have been dismal enough in the sunlight, but now it was disheartening. The valley back yonder had been fat with the vigorous young summer; here only bunch grass grew, and no brush was in sight as far as they could see to where the descending curtains of the rain shut out the world.

A fire was out of the question.   Chilled with the
night's long drenching, they mounted and rode
away at a jog trot, with their backs to the drowned
dawn, while Baptiste muttered weird French oaths
in his streaming whiskers.

After hours they found themselves in a gumbo
plain from whence, at intervals, grotesquely
carven buttes soared flat-topped into the soppy
haze.   They were obliged to proceed at a walk
now, for the earth was spongy and the hoofs of
the horses popped and sucked as they floundered
on.   No wood all that day; and when the dark
came on, once more the men bivouacked in the
mud and drench.

The rain ceased in the night and morning
came with a golden sun that set the drear land
steaming.   Close on noon they topped the gully-
torn divide between the feeders of the Big and
Little Missouri, and gazing westward they saw
afar the valley of the latter stream, a tangle of
ragged gulches and rain-sculptured buttes.   During the afternoon Baptiste's rifle rolled a mountain sheep from a butte top, and that evening
they feasted by the Little Missouri where a plum
thicket furnished fuel and a patch of slough grass
offered a good night's grazing for the animals.

Up and off at the first light, they crossed the
river at the expense of another thorough soaking, for the stream was swollen with the recent
rains; and when the horses plunged under in mid-

current, the riders were forced to take to the water, gripping the saddle horn with one hand. But the soaking mattered little so long as their screw-topped horns kept their powder dry. After hours of hard going in torrent-carved gulches, they emerged upon a lonesome upland and struck out northwest, crossing a number of creeks during the day, all of which flowed in a northerly direction; and they knew that they were now within the drainage area of the Yellowstone River.

On the second day from the crossing of the Little Missouri they began to follow the rugged valley of a small stream that led them in two more days into the valley of the Yellowstone. Game, grass, and wood were plentiful now; but Indians might also be plentiful, for the Assiniboines, who had proven themselves unfriendly to Henry's party the year before, were known to wander over this region as far as the mouth of the Powder, where Absaroka, the Country of the Crows, began. Once more Jed and Baptiste travelled by night; and without encountering any further difficulties, they came in the white dawn of the third day to the junction of the two great rivers.

An hour later, the gates of Henry's fort on the south bank of the Missouri, four miles above the mouth of the Yellowstone, swung open and the two horsemen, bedraggled with their recent swim, rode into the enclosure and dismounted amid a throng of trappers clamoring for news frcm Ashley. A tall, slender man, with keen gray-blue eyes and the quiet, confident bearing of one who is born to command, pushed his way through the gathering of eager men; and for the first time Jedediah Smith and Major Henry met. Together these two withdrew to one of the larger log cabins of the post, leaving Baptiste to enlarge and embellish, in the picturesque mongrel tongue of the French *voyageur,* the tale of the battle with the Rees and the long cross-country ride from the mouth of the Grand.

VI

IT was indeed a discouraging situation that
Major Henry faced that day; for it seemed
that his business venture with General Ashley had
been doomed to failure from the very beginning.
The series of misfortunes, as we have seen, had
begun before his northbound expedition of the
preceding spring had passed beyond the limit of
the States. Near Fort Osage, in the State of
Missouri, a keelboat with all its cargo had gone
to the bottom of the river. Then, on the last lap
of the arduous journey to the Yellowstone, he had
lost his horses to the Assiniboines. Only recently
he had returned from his defeat by the Blackfeet,
in the region of the Great Falls, to his post near
the junction of the rivers, determined to push on
again as soon as the second party should join him.
With this in view he had sent an express to Ashley
with the news of his urgent need; and now came
these riders from Ashley, asking help of one who
had been unable to help himself! Such are the
occasional ironies of circumstance that sometimes
make misfortune seem a mysterious and malevo-
lent personality.

Henry moved with characteristic promptness. Leaving twenty of his men in possession of the post, he set out by keelboat next morning with the balance of his party.   Jed and Baptiste went with him.

Of all the primitive modes of travel, none is more delightful than down-stream drifting when the June floods run; and now the distant mountains were feeding the river with their melting snows.   When the winds are light or blow astern, this means of overcoming distance is the next best thing to standing on a magic carpet and wishing the miles away.   A great calm had followed the wide-sweeping rains, and the keelboat kept the boiling current like a conscious being well aware of its trail.   Through the slow lapse of the June days the men had nothing to do but to smoke and tell yarns.

The story of the Blackfoot battle was told and retold until the latest version was scarcely to be regarded as a collection of related individual accounts, but rather as a rudimentary work of art whose author was the whole group consciousness. This " gentle art of lying," the alleged passing of which was once eloquently bemoaned by Oscar Wilde, reached a high degree of development among the wandering bands of the Early West. But " lying " is far too harsh a word; rather let us call it the process of finding a thread of reason running through the apparent unreasonableness of circumstance; of making beauty by the simple means of shifting the relationship between facts that in themselves appear unbeautiful. Thus do men seek to put their world in order about them, that life may still be understandable and dear.

And there was another story that Henry's men did not weary of telling from many angles and with many sidelights during the idle days of drifting. Already the tale had taken artistic form under the manipulation of the group consciousness, though it had not yet reached the final rounded version in which it would become familiar throughout the wilderness wherever two men might share the warmth of smouldering embers. It was the story of Fink, Carpenter and Talbeau.[1] Only recently these men had seen its climax; yet already it was charged with something of the remoteness and the mystery of doom.

There were those who remembered the old days on the Ohio and the Mississippi when the mutual love of the three boatmen was a byword in all the river ports. Fink was a " wild Irishman," a famous joker and a terrible fighter, with the body of a Hercules and a face that suggested a bulldog. Men laughed freely at his jokes in those good old days, for it was well known that whoever neglected to laugh must be prepared for instant battle. Carpenter was tall, slenderly but powerfully built, and a blond. He smiled much, talked lit-

[1] *The Western Monthly Review.* Cincinnati, 1830. Vol. III.

tle, and fought well with a show of good nature that was disconcerting. Talbeau was a small man, but one who had once seen the three fight their way through a crowded dance hall on the lower Mississippi, spoke highly of the little man's terrier-like effectiveness in a scrimmage. Fink and Carpenter were expert marksmen, and often each would shoot a whisky cup from the other's head at a distance of forty yards by way of demonstrating both their skill and their faith in each other.

These three cronies had joined Henry's expedition of the preceding year, and had spent the winter with nine other men among the Blood Indians at the mouth of the Musselshell. There Fink and Carpenter had fallen out at last over a half-breed girl, and had come to blows despite the desperate efforts of Talbeau to pacify them. The fight that followed was stubborn and long, but Carpenter had won, owing less to his strength and skill, perhaps, than to his coolness. Fink was not the man to forgive, and he had never before known defeat.

Spring came, the Musselshell party returned to the fort near the mouth of the Yellowstone, and there the quarrel was renewed. Once more Talbeau strove to pacify his friends, and with apparent success. At the little man's suggestion, the two big men agreed to join in the old rite of friendship — the shooting of the cup. A coin was tossed for the first shot, which fell to Fink. Now calling Talbeau aside, Carpenter willed his gun, flint, powder horn, knife and blankets to the little man, who laughingly accepted the bequest, remarking that Fink couldn't miss a target if he tried. Whether or not Fink missed his target was still a question among the tellers of the tale. What he hit was a spot between the eyes of his old friend.[1]

So in the enforced idleness of the down-stream journey, the men whiled away the hours by spinning yarns:

> Looped yarns wherein the veteran spinners vied
> To color with a lie more glorified
> Some thread that had veracity enough —
> Spun straightway out of life's own precious stuff
> That each had scutched and heckled in the raw.

And often in the nights of drifting, when the men lay huddled together on deck, gazing at the stars or watching the shadowy shore forge slowly to the rear, some French *voyageur* would strike up a well-known tune on a fiddle, setting the band to singing and causing the wolves and coyotes to yip and yammer among the bluffs. And once Major Henry himself, who loved the violin and handled it with considerable skill, played a weird air that sobbed like a woman, yet was very sweet to hear, somehow. And the men were silent, marvelling

[1] The complete story is to be found in my narrative poem, "The Song of Three Friends," Macmillan, 1919.

that he who played there in the starlight was the same Henry whom they had seen calm in battle and of whom so many tales of daring were told.

It was near the end of the third week in June when the party, having drifted by the mouth of the Cannonball River, began to dread the passing of the Ree towns; and all tales were forgotten in the general discussion of that coming event. There were those who pointed out how the high bluff above the upper village, and at the foot of which the main current then ran, would be swarming with Indians prepared to rake the keelboat's deck with a plunging fire; and others saw the wooded island below the lower village belching rifle smoke and impossible to pass. And what of the four hundred yards of pickets between those two strategic points? Over and over the imagined battle was fought; but when, in mid-afternoon of the next day, the keelboat swept about a righthand bend and swirled down a westward stretch with the upper Ree town to starboard, while the men gripped their cocked rifles, nothing serious happened. Dogs barked, villagers crowded on the lodge tops, and a band of unarmed braves, running down the beach, signalled with buffalo robes by way of indicating their keen desire to trade and their very benevolent intentions. But the keelboat swept on with the strong June current, and soon the babble of the towns had died out astern. Having drifted all night long, at sunset of the following day the party came to Ashley's camp near the mouth of the Cheyenne.

We may be sure that there was great talk that night about the fires; and though the dominant theme was defeat, the glare of the embers revealed the weathered faces of many who were destined to great victories. At this distance in time the light upon their features is dim, but the memory of their achievements is like a torch flaring in a gloom for those who are familiar with that period. First of all, there was Andrew Henry, whose adventures in the region of the Three Forks and beyond the Great Divide lead one back to the days of Manuel Lisa and the men of Lewis and Clark. Near him sat Ashley, whose future explorations on the upper waters of the Colorado would fix his name in our history. Yonder was James Bridger, a lad of nineteen years, who would be the first to look upon Great Salt Lake, and whose career, then just beginning, would outlast the fur trade and the Sioux Wars, ending peacefully nearly sixty years later on a Missouri farm. The powerfully built, gray-bearded man was Hugh Glass, the memory of whose amazing adventures would preserve for posterity the record of Henry's important westbound expedition in the fall of that year. Yonder sat Fitzpatrick, soon to be widely known among the tribes of the West as " The Chief of the Withered Hand "; and not far away was Etienne Provost. Both of these

have been credited with the discovery of South
Pass; but the former was doubtless the first white
man to travel through that important gateway to
the land beyond the Rockies.   In the glow of another fire sat William L. Sublette, a tall man with
blue eyes, sandy hair, and a Roman nose.   He
would be the first to take wagons to the mountains
over the great natural road later to be known as
the Oregon Trail.   Here was Edward Rose, yonder David Jackson and Louis Vasquez — names
to conjure with in those days of mighty men.   But
more important than any yet named was the slender, taciturn man of twenty-five who had just returned from his hazardous journey to the Yellowstone.   He would be the first to travel the great
central route to the Pacific, the first American to
reach California by land.

These men, with many others, who talked about
the fires that night and are now forgotten, were
the real explorers of the West between the route
of Lewis and Clark and the northern boundary of
New Mexico and Arizona.   During the next two
decades, this body of men would scatter over the
whole Trans-Missouri country.

During that evening General Ashley and Major
Henry decided to move the united parties down
stream to the mouth of the Teton, there to wait
for the reinforcements that they hoped would be
sent up-stream by the military authorities at Fort
Atkinson.   During Jedediah Smith's absence, the

keelboat *Yellowstone* had dropped down stream
to Atkinson, bearing the seriously wounded men
of Ashley's command and a message from the defeated General to Colonel Leavenworth, then
commander of that post. Coincident with the arrival of the keelboat at the fort, the tragic tale of
another disaster to American traders came from
Pryor's Fork of the Yellowstone. There in May,
Jones and Immel who, as we have seen, had set
out in advance of Henry in the spring of 1822,
had encountered a superior number of hostile
Blackfeet and had been killed, together with five
of their men. The loss of property was reckoned
at $15,000 — a large sum in those days.

Moved by this accumulation of misfortune,
Leavenworth acted promptly, and was now already pushing northward to punish the Rees and
to render the riverway safe for American traders
and trappers.

During the next day after the arrival of Henry's party at the mouth of the Cheyenne, Jedediah Smith, with one companion, started out on
another journey, being chosen to take to St. Louis
the furs that Henry's men had collected during the
previous fall and spring. One of the most striking facts in this man's short and wonderful career
was his ceaseless activity. His entry into the fur
trade may be likened to a plunge into an irresist-
ible current that should bear him swiftly and far,
and from which the release could be through death

alone.   Such facts in human lives are not to be regarded as matters of chance, but rather as mani-
festations of temperament.   Curious, capable,
fearless, and self-contained, Smith was never the
man to wait for events.   He went forth eagerly
to meet them.   Such ever are the splendid way-
farers of this world.

VII

THE LEAVENWORTH CAMPAIGN

ON June 22nd, that is to say, at about the time when Major Henry reached the mouth of the Cheyenne, Colonel Leavenworth had started north from Fort Atkinson with six companies of the Sixth United States Infantry, consisting of two hundred twenty men, three keelboats, including the *Yellowstone* sent down by Ashley, and two six-pound cannon. Five days later Joshua Pilcher of the Missouri Fur Company, with sixty trappers and two keelboats, upon one of which a small howitzer was mounted, overtook the military expedition and joined forces with it. On July 6th another keelboat was procured from a descending party of trappers.

Owing to the very high water and continuous headwinds, the advance of the combined parties was slow. During the night of the 8th of July a terrific storm of wind and rain, such as all prairie dwellers know, drove the *Yellowstone* from her moorings and wrecked her on a sandbar, where all night long in the violent downpour her crew struggled to save her cargo from the raging river. Once again, as the more superstitious

voyageurs were, doubtless, not slow to note, it was
Ashley's property that had been chosen for misfortune.   Plainly, luck was no friend to the General!   Two days were lost in hauling the keelboat
ashore and repairing it.

On July 19th the expedition arrived at Fort
Recovery, situated on the island that lies opposite
the present town of Oacoma, South Dakota; and
there two small bands of Yankton and Teton
Sioux joined the whites.   Nine days later, the
forces under Leavenworth were further increased
by two hundred Saone and Uncpapa Sioux, who
had reasons of their own for wishing to move
against the Rees under circumstances apparently
so favorable.   The last day of the month was
spent in waiting for another large band of Sioux
Indians who had sent runners to announce their intention of joining the expedition.

It was not until the first of August that Leavenworth reached the camp of Ashley and Henry,
who, having succeeded in procuring a supply of
horses from the Sioux at the mouth of the Teton,
had moved on a short distance down stream, intending to proceed overland to the Yellowstone if
the military forces failed to arrive within a reasonable time.   There were now but eighty men
in their party, and these were placed at the dis-
posal of Colonel Leavenworth, who proceeded at
once to organize the motley collection of fighting
men under his command into a military body.

The result was styled "The Missouri Legion."

During the first week of August, the progress of the expedition was considerably retarded by the whims of the Indian allies, some of whom were inclined to indulge in dog-feasts while the United States Army waited in advance, and others in large numbers insisted upon being ferried across the river now and then — an operation costing considerable time and effort. However, on the 8th of August the Legion, being then at a point twenty-five miles below the Ree towns, succeeded at last in getting together, and the general advance began. Considering the time, the place, and the strength of the foe, it was truly a formidable force that Colonel Leavenworth viewed that day, and it must have made a pretty show as it moved northward. One hundred forty long-haired and bearded trappers in the picturesque semi-savage garb of the wilderness; two hundred twenty United States regulars in army blue; four hundred Sioux Indians, splendid in war-paint and feathers, about half of them armed with bows, lances and war-clubs; and in addition to these, a fleet of six keelboats! Surely now the Rees were about to pay dearly for their treachery!

At sunset the Legion went into camp ten miles nearer to its objective, and early in the morning of the 9th it was on the march again. "During the day," says the Colonel in his report to the War Department, "we continually received the

most strange and contradictory accounts from
our Indians.   It appeared that there were several
Sioux living with the Aricaras and who had in-
termarried with them.   They were sent for, to
come out and see their friends, who were coming,
as the Sioux said, to smoke and make peace with
the Aricaras.   Some said that the villages were
strongly fortified and furnished with ditches as
deep as a man's chin when standing in them.   At
other times it was said that the Aricaras were so
confident that the Sioux were coming to make
peace with them that they had taken down their
defences and that there was nothing to defend
them but their dirt lodges.   Nothing appeared
certain but that the Aricaras were still in their
villages.   These contradictory stories, which were
told by the Sioux, had the effect to create sus-
picions of their fidelity.   It was also reported
(and there was too much reason to believe it true)
that the Saones and Uncpapas, who were combined, had determined, in case we were defeated,
to join the Aricaras."

Surely a military commander has seldom been
placed in a more precarious situation than that of
Leavenworth; and to make matters worse, it became more and more apparent that Joshua Pilcher
was concerned far less with the success of Leavenworth's expedition than with the failure of Ashley's enterprise.   Through a wily Frenchman of
his party, one Simoneau, who seems to have been

the only interpreter available to Leavenworth in his relations with the Sioux, Pilcher evidently left nothing undone that might increase his own prestige with the Indian allies, at the same time discrediting Ashley and embarrassing the unfortunate Colonel. The following incident of the advance, as told by Leavenworth in his official report, is typical: " Mr. Pilcher soon came to me with an Indian whom he reported to be an Aricara, and said that he had delivered himself up and claimed protection. I dismounted and disarmed the Indian, and placed him under guard and gave his arms to a Sioux who was destitute. It afterwards appeared that Major Pilcher's Aricara prisoner was a Sioux who belonged to the Major's command! "

It can scarcely be questioned that the Sioux very soon came to regard the whole affair as rather a lark and the white soldiers as the butt of a good joke. At no time was Colonel Leavenworth able to control them. Having been placed on the flanks of the advancing force, with instructions to keep those positions, " they were soon out of sight " in the direction of the villages. When about three miles from their objective, the soldiers heard brisk firing ahead, and soon met some of the Sioux returning pell mell with a few captured Ree horses. At this juncture, Pilcher turned up with a report that the enemy had met the Sioux near the villages " and had not only maintained their ground against the Sioux, but had driven them back." He therefore insisted " that it was highly important to press forward one or two companies to support the Sioux, or the consequences would probably be prejudicial." The soldiery immediately " set out on a run " and soon the Legion was within striking distance of the foe. But when the men were deployed in battle formation, nothing happened, owing to the unfortunate fact that the unruly Indian allies were ahead and obstructed the line of fire!

The enemy now withdrew into the villages, and the Sioux, who had succeeded in killing a few Rees, decided that the proper moment had arrived for playing the not too edifying game of " White Bear." " This consisted," so the Colonel tells us, " of placing the skin of that animal over the shoulders of a Sioux who walked upon his hands and knees and endeavored to imitate the bear in his motions by walking around and smelling the dead bodies. Sometimes he would cut off small pieces of the flesh and eat it."

By the time the Sioux had tired of their game, and when the keelboats had at last arrived with the artillery, night was approaching and the Colonel decided to postpone further operations until the next day, August 10th.

The great day arrived; but when the soldiers and trappers had taken advantageous positions about the towns, it was remarked that " our In-

dian allies were very much scattered in the rear."
However, the artillery opened fire. The first
shot killed the great Ree chief, Gray Eyes, and
the second brought down the Ree medicine pole.
This seemed a very good beginning, indeed. A
party under Major Ketchum was now ordered to
advance and did so —" until ordered to halt."
Being then within three hundred yards of the
lower village, it occurred to the Major that the
guns of his heroes " had been loaded for a considerable time," and that it was " desirable to discharge them." (The guns, not the heroes!)
The guns were thereupon fired — with what effect
we are not told.

At this juncture Leavenworth became convinced
that it would be well to examine the Ree defences,
thanks to a certain Mr. McDonald who had spent
some time in the villages. It was Mr. McDonald's opinion that the defences were so strong and
the Rees so confident in their strength that " in
case an assault were made, every squaw would
count her coup (that is, kill a man)." " With a
view to ascertaining the strength of the fortifica-
tions," continues the Colonel, " I thought of making an assault upon an acute angle of the upper
town, which I could approach within one hundred
steps under cover of a hill. Accordingly Major
Ketchum was ordered to advance. General Ashley with his command (trappers) was also ordered to advance. He did so in the most gallant

manner. He promptly took possession of a ravine within twenty steps of the lower town and
maintained a spirited action, well calculated to
assist us in our design upon the upper town, by
making a diversion in our favor."

By this time, however, the mood of the Sioux
seems to have dwindled from martial to bucolic.
" For when all other things were ready," com-
plains the sorely tried Colonel, " I was mortified
exceedingly to learn from Mr. Pilcher that no
assistance could be obtained from the Sioux in consequence of their being so deeply engaged in gathering corn " in the fields of the Rees!   (One can
scarcely blame them, for it was the time of roasting ears, the eating of which they naturally found
much more pleasurable than fighting!)   Leavenworth thereupon decided not to proceed with the
examination of the enemy defences; for, having
gained the desired information, he would be compelled to fall back under cover of the hill, there
to organize the attack; and the Sioux, being likely
to mistake that strategic maneuver for defeat,
might join the Rees.   Furthermore, some of the
enemy, at this time, created a counter-diversion
by issuing from the towns and occupying a ravine
in the rear of " our men on the hill."   So the
reconnaissance failed.

Leavenworth now went in search of Pilcher and
found him and his men " lying in a hollow behind
the hill."   After some conversation with the leis-

urely gentleman, the Colonel decided " to direct
Simoneau to go as near the village as he could
with safety, hail the Aricaras and tell them they
were fools not to come out and speak with the
whites." Simoneau hailed the Rees twice, and
then said that the wind blew so hard he couldn't
make himself heard. Whereupon the Colonel remarked " that it was a matter of no consequence."

In the meanwhile both the upper and lower villages had been receiving a desultory shelling from
the six-pounders and the howitzer; but, upon
learning that only thirty-nine rounds of ammunition remained, the Colonel commanded the artillery to cease firing in order to save the remaining
shot for a general assault upon the towns which
he planned to make. He then notified the Sioux,
still hotly engaged with the serried ranks of the
corn, that he wished them to withdraw. They
obeyed, owing, no doubt, to the fact that they had
gathered all the roasting ears they could carry.
Both Ketchum and Ashley were recalled from
their advanced positions, and a party was organized to invade the enemy's cornfields " to obtain
subsistence for our men, several of whom, par-
ticularly General Ashley's command, had not had
any provisions for two days."

The Colonel, having every reason to believe
that the assault upon the armies of the green corn
would be prosecuted with conspicuous gallantry,
retired to the cabin of his keelboat, probably to

meditate in quiet upon his victories. It was now mid-afternoon. " Very soon afterwards," he tells us, " Mr. Pilcher came into my cabin and apparently with great alarm informed me that Captain Riley was attacked. I was very glad to hear it, and immediately went out to send him support. But behold! Captain Riley and all our men were very quietly coming in without the least knowledge of any attack being made upon them. Mr. Pilcher remarked that this report was unfortunately too much like the case of his Aricara prisoner! "

An hour later, while conferring with General Ashley concerning operations that were to follow, Leavenworth saw a Sioux and an Aricara holding a conversation on the plain in front of the villages. He sent for Pilcher and told him that the Sioux and Rees were holding a parley and asked him " to go and see to it." Pilcher moved off with his interpreter, Simoneau, toward the place indicated. Then, " casting my eye up the hills in our rear," continues the Colonel's report, " I discovered that they were covered with the retreating Sioux, and I soon had reason to know that they were all going off. I immediately mounted my horse and went after Mr. Pilcher to be present at the parley with the Sioux and Aricaras."

The Rees now asked pity for their women and children, and said they did not want to be fired upon any more. Gray Eyes, who had caused all the mischief, was dead. The Ree chiefs wished to talk and make peace. Leavenworth was quite ready to talk, and the chiefs came. " Do with us as you please," said they, " but do not fire any more guns at us. We are all in tears." The Colonel replied that they must make up General Ashley's losses, and give up five principal men of their tribe as a guarantee of good conduct in the future. The chiefs agreed to restore everything possible. Their horses had been taken by the Sioux and killed in great numbers. They had no horses to give, but they would return all the guns they could find and the articles of property they had received from General Ashley. They would even return the hats! Also, they would give five of their number as hostages. Accordingly, a treaty was signed — but not by the principal chiefs of the tribe, as Pilcher, with some asperity, pointed out to the Colonel. As to General Ashley's property, three rifles, one horse and sixteen buffalo robes were returned. When the hostages arrived, Leavenworth refused to receive them, as they were evidently men of no importance.

Thus the farce went on, Pilcher constantly playing at cross purposes with the Colonel, until, during the night of the 12th of August, the Rees fled from their villages — all except one feeble old squaw, the mother of the dead chief, Gray Eyes. There was now nothing left for Leavenworth to do but to march away. During the night of his departure, contrary to his orders, the towns were fired by parties unknown, though suspicion seemed to point to certain men of the Missouri Fur Company.

On the 23rd of August, Pilcher, then at Fort Recovery, addressed the following letter to Colonel Leavenworth: " I am well aware that humanity and philanthropy are mighty shields for you against those who are entirely ignorant of the disposition and character of the Indians; but with those who have experienced the fatal and ruinous consequences of their treachery and barbarity these considerations will avail nothing. You came to restore peace and tranquillity to the country, and to leave an impression which would insure its continuance. Your operations have been such as to produce the contrary effect, and to impress the different tribes with the greatest contempt for the American character. You came (to use your own language) ' to open and make good this great road '; instead of which you have, by the imbecility of your conduct and operations, created and left impassable barriers."

So ended the first campaign of the United States Army against the Indians of the Plains. The forces under Leavenworth's command, including the trappers and the Sioux, had numbered slightly over one thousand. The Ree villages at that time contained about seven hundred warriors and something over three thousand old men, squaws and children. Two white men had been wounded and two of the Sioux killed, while the Rees had lost no more than thirty, some of whom were women and children.   The cost of the campaign to the United States Government was computed at $2,038.24.

It was a Gilbert and Sullivan opera without the rhymes and the music, Pilcher playing the rôle of the heavy villain.   But perhaps Colonel Leavenworth should not be too greatly blamed for the fiasco.   His conduct at the battles of Chippewa and Niagara Falls in the War of 1812 amply proves that he had no lack of courage; and we have George Catlin's word for it that the manner of his death, some years later, was noble.   In his campaign against the Rees he was the victim of commercial rivalry.

Nevertheless, one wonders what might have been the result if an officer like Crook had been in command.   Or Custer!   Fancy Pilcher, or any other man, playing at ducks and drakes with him who humbled the Cheyenne on the Washita, and died with all his men on the bluffs along the Little Big Horn!

VIII

WESTWARD BY THE GRAND

NOW that the Ree campaign was over, General Ashley returned to St. Louis, and Major Henry, with an inadequate number of horses that had been purchased from the Sioux, set out by way of the Grand River valley for his post at the mouth of the Yellowstone. Jedediah Smith, who had but recently returned from St. Louis, accompanied the expedition.

Two hundred men had gone north in the two Ashley-Henry parties of 1822 and 1823; and now, in mid-August of the latter year, the number had dwindled to one hundred, counting those left by Henry at the mouth of the Yellowstone. But hardship and calamity had tested these; the frailer spirits had been eliminated by natural selection; and it was the pick of the fur trade that rode away from the Missouri in the waning summer. Thus the resistance of the Rees, that in itself might seem an insignificant episode, is raised to a position of historical importance when viewed in relation to the westward race-movement; for that tribe of savages had acted as the principal agent in a sifting process, out of which should come sturdy spirits fit to lead the van of the Aryan peoples on the last lap of the long journey from Mesopotamia to where the sun goes down in the Pacific.

However, it was not as conscious forerunners of civilization that these men went forth; and that they should ever be regarded as benefactors of the human race could not have occurred to the generality of them. The two great forces that have caused all folk-wanderings impelled them — the economic urge and the perennial human curiosity that is basic in the love of adventure. The leaders, with the single exception of Jedediah Smith, were doubtless in their own estimation merely traders and trappers, out for the precious beaver pelts with which to buy what no man ever purchased at a price — happiness; and the rank and file, receiving from $150 to $300 per year, were lured on by the witchery of danger and the free life of the wilderness. Their heroism was a mere by-product; yet it alone has enriched the race, while the beaver fur, that seemed all important at the time, has returned to dust.

In "Lord Jim" Joseph Conrad has the following passage, which, though it refers to wanderers on the Seven Seas, is peculiarly applicable to these early explorers of the Far West: "To us, their less tried successors, they appear magnified, not as agents of trade, but as instruments of a recorded destiny, pushing out into the unknown in obedience to an inward voice, to an impulse beating in the blood, to a dream of the future."

Our common human nature may be greater than we know!

Were it possible for us now to look backward (unaided by the imagination), and glimpse with the naked eye those eighty men pushing westward in the broiling day amid the dust kicked up by the sweating pack animals, we would probably consider them somewhat grotesque in appearance. Some of those who had come up with Ashley that spring were still clad in the garb of civilization (sadly in need of patches!). Others of the same band had already been forced to discard a portion of their original clothing, and now wore an incongruous combination of Indian and white man's clothing. Those who had wintered at the mouth of the Yellowstone had long since shed the clothes with which they had started from St. Louis, and, having adopted the whole Indian costume, with the exception, perhaps, of a blue cotton shirt procured from the keelboats, could scarcely be distinguished, at a distance of a hundred yards, from the wild natives. Many of these wore deerskin leggings that left the hips and thighs bare save for a cloth that was folded around the loins and tucked under the girdle. From this girdle were suspended leather bags containing hunting knife, hatchet, flint and steel, pipe and tobacco, or any smaller articles of personal use which, in the jargon of the trapper, were known as " fixins " or " possibles." A buckskin belt, slung over the left shoulder and under the right arm, carried the ammunition for the long muzzle-loading rifle. Vari-colored fringes, embroideries done in beads and hair, dyed feathers and a variety of other savage ornaments set off this strange attire. Some were still wearing boots and shoes, but most, either through necessity or whim, had adopted the moccasin wrought of a single piece of dressed buckskin sewed from heel to ankle with deer sinew and gathered from toe to instep. Large red or blue cotton handkerchiefs, tied in the shape of a turban, served most of these men for headgear.[1]

But however hit-and-miss these men might appear, there was nothing haphazard about the manner of their progress; for as a result of his experiences in the wilderness, Major Henry had worked out a complete technique for the moving of bodies of men through hostile Indian country. The organization of the band, the duties of each unit, the order of march, and the method of making camp were as much a matter of rigid plan as was the case with a Roman legion under Cæsar. General Ashley has left us the following account of such arrangements:[2]

" In the organization of a party, say from sixty to eighty men, four of the most confidential and

[1] Encyclopedia of St. Louis, quoted by Chittenden.
[2] Chittenden, " History of the American Fur Trade." Vol. III.

experienced of the number are selected to aid in the command; the rest are divided into messes of eight or ten. A suitable man is also appointed at the head of each mess, whose duty it is to make known the wants of his mess, receive supplies for them, make distributions, watch over their conduct, enforce orders, etc. The party thus organized, each man receives the horses and mules allotted to him, their equipage, and the packs which his mules are to carry. Every article so disposed of is entered in a book kept for that purpose. When the party reaches the Indian country, great order and vigilance in the discharge of their duty are required of every man. A variety of circumstances confines the march very often to the borders of large water courses. When that is the case, it is found convenient and safe, when the ground will admit, to locate our camps (which are generally laid off in a square) so as to make the river form one line, and include as much ground in it as may be sufficient for the whole number of horses, allowing for each a range of thirty feet in diameter.

" On the arrival of the party at their camping place, the position of each mess is pointed out, where their packs, saddles, etc., are taken off, and with these a breastwork is immediately put up to cover them from a night attack by Indians. The horses are then watered and delivered to the horse-guards, who keep them on the best grass outside and near the encampment, where they graze until sunset. Then each man brings his horses within the limits of the camp, exchanges the light halter for the other more substantial one, sets his stakes, which are placed at the distance of thirty feet from each other, and secures his horses to them. This range of thirty feet, in addition to the grass the horse has collected outside the camp, will be sufficient for him during the night.

"After these regulations, the proceedings for the night are pretty much the same as are practiced in military camps. At daylight (when in dangerous parts of the country) two or more men are mounted on horseback and sent to examine ravines, woods, hills, and other places within striking distance of the camp, where Indians might secrete themselves, before the men are allowed to leave their breastworks to make the necessary morning arrangements for the march. When these spies report favorably, the horses are taken outside the camp, delivered to the horseguard, and allowed to graze until the party has breakfasted, and are ready for saddling.

"In the line of march, each mess takes its choice of position in the line according to its activity in making ready to move. The mess first ready to march moves up in the rear of an officer, who marches in the front of the party, and takes its choice of position; and so they all proceed until the line is formed.   In that way they march the whole of that day.   Spies are sent out several miles ahead to examine the country in the vicinity of the route, and others are kept at the distance of a half mile or more from the party, as the lay of the ground seems to require, in front, in rear and on the flanks.   In making discoveries of Indians, they communicate the same by signals, or otherwise, to the commanding officer, who makes his arrangements accordingly."

In this manner the band had moved two days up the Grand River, making fairly good time in spite of the fact that most of the men were afoot, the horses purchased from the Sioux being needed for the packs of merchandise brought up in Ashley's keelboats.   It yet lacked two hours until sunset when, weary with the long day's journey in the broiling sun, the party rounded a bend and saw, a little way ahead, a lone horse, unsaddled and tethered, peacefully nipping the lush grass of a pleasant knoll that flanked the stream. Sitting, nearby, a gray-bearded, powerfully built man was leisurely skinning a buck deer.   From the lower limbs of a neighboring tree hung three antelope, already dressed.

A cheer went up from the hungry men in the van, and, running down the column, set the pack horses nickering.   The old man was Hugh Glass, the chief hunter of the party, whose duty it was to ride well in advance of his comrades and have fresh meat waiting on a likely camping spot when the band should come up in the evening.

The place is soon filled with the bustle and noise of eighty men and fifty horses. The packers, halting their animals on three sides of a square, the fourth being the river, uncinch the horses and place their packs on the ground so as to form a breastwork. The horses roll in the cool grass, grunting and whinnying by way of expressing their satisfaction. Now the horse-guards take charge of the herd, leading it to water and good grazing outside the camp. Meanwhile, details from each mess are gathering dry wood and building fires, while others are portioning out the meat and preparing it for supper. Those who have no special duties today have already stripped and are splashing and laughing boisterously in a pool nearby, like the light-hearted boys that many of them are. Now the kettles are bubbling over the fires and the pleasant smell of meat is in the air. The sun drops slowly behind the bluffs and a grateful shade falls cool and blue along the valley. Now at last the meal is ready, and the men fall to with Homeric appetites.

Pipes were out and lit, and some of the men had begun to sing, when a scout came galloping up with a tale of Rees. He had caught sight of two Indians peering down upon him from a bluff top an hour since; and he was convinced that they were the spies of a war party that planned to

attack under cover of the darkness. The singing
stopped. The horse-guards were called in, and
the horses securely staked within the hollow
square, while the men were assigned to their
places behind the baggage. The fires were put
out and the soft starry August gloom deepened
over the camp. One man in each mess having
been detailed for guard duty, the rest were per-
mitted to sleep with their loaded rifles beside
them.

Hour after hour passed, and still, as the watch-
men peered into the darkness, nothing moved, for
it was a windless night. They heard the nipping
and blowing of the contented horses. Now and
then wolves howled or an owl screeched. The
sleepy stars swarmed westward, and the Dipper
pointed midnight on the polar dial. Still nothing happened. The sleepy watches grumbled to
each other and in low undertones said uncompli-
mentary things of Indians in general, of the Rees
in particular, and of Colonel Leavenworth for
having failed to make a clean job of the late campaign.

Another hour passed. Then one of the horses,
with head held high, began to snort and blow.
The whole herd stopped grazing and, with ears
pricked forward, stared up the starlit slope to the
southward toward where a thicket of plum and
bullberry loomed black. Somewhere not far off

a horse neighed, and the nervous herd answered in unison.

Scarcely had each sentry wakened his mess with the one word, " Injuns," when there broke out of the hush the running crack of rifle fire and the *whee-oo-plunk* of a flight of arrows falling all about the camp. Some trapper swore in a shrill note of pain. Then the mingled howl of many savage voices swept down the hillside, and with the rumble of galloping hoofs the attack was launched upon the trappers.

Howgh! Howgh! Howgh! Howgh! On came the howling riders, shadowy in the starlight and seeming the more formidable for their vagueness. Scarcely heard above the tumult of the terrified horses, some of which had been struck by arrows, the men behind the baggage were shouting to each other to wait until the foe was close. Only three or four rifles went off prematurely.

Surely in a moment more the charge would sweep right over the camp!

The whole breastwork of baggage blazed and roared. The shadowy ponies in front reared screaming. Some collapsed like figures in a dream, and through the spreading smoke of the rifles the trappers, hastily reloading, saw the scattered war-party flying back up the slope. With a yell the white men leaped over the baggage and, rushing in among the fallen Indian ponies, " lifted

the hair " of the dead and wounded Rees.   They
came back with a half dozen scalps.

When the excitement had abated and an examination of the camp was made, two trappers, Anderson and Neil, were found dead.   Also, the old
veteran, he of the many tales, coolly announced
that he had an arrow in his " hump-ribs " that
would have to be " butchered out," as he expressed it —an operation which, after lighting his
pipe, he underwent without an outcry.   Several
of the horses had been wounded and some would
be lame.

In the morning, while the herd was grazing outside the camp and the cooks were getting breakfast ready, Neil and Anderson were buried, the
ceremony consisting of a prayer by Jed Smith,
who, according to the concensus of opinion, seemed
most likely to be heard.   Very little was said
about the two for whom a permanent camp had
been made there by the Grand.   They had been
" out of luck " and they were " rubbed out."   So
it was.

All that day, and for two days thereafter, the
party pushed on up the river valley, encountering
no more Indians.   Evidently the Rees had decided that Henry's men asked too high a price
for their animals, and had therefore gone in
search of a cheaper market.   The progress of
the band was a bit slower now, for the wounded
horses did well to follow bare-backed, and their

packs were distributed among the rest of the herd that had been heavily laden from the start.

It was not until evening of the third day after the attack that misfortune came again. The band had been toiling all day under a blazing sun, hoping to reach the forks of the Grand for the night encampment; and as the time for halting drew near, the men began to watch eagerly for Hugh Glass. Bend after bend was rounded, and each bend brought a fresh disappointment. The men began to grumble. What could be the matter with old Glass? Did he expect them to march all night without supper? At length as the sun was nearing the horizon Major Henry called a halt, and the men, sullen at the prospect of supper without fresh meat, began to make camp. They had not gone far with their preparations, however, when young Bridger, who, with Fitzpatrick, had been riding in advance that day, came up at a brisk gallop; and the trappers, noting his haste, leaped to the conclusion that they were in for another encounter with the Rees.

But it was a very different tale that Bridger had to tell. He and Fitzpatrick, while riding near the forks of the river two hours since, had pushed through a bullberry thicket near a spring and had come suddenly upon old Glass lying as though dead, with a bloody hunting knife beside him. Not far away lay the carcass of a grizzly bear. The old man's face was " all scraped off,"

as Bridger put it; " and when we lifted him, one
of his legs went wobbly and he groaned." It was
evident that the old hunter had been taken by
surprise and had not been able to " set his trigger," for his gun was still loaded and the great
gashes in the bear's neck, chest and belly showed
how Hugh had fought. Doubtless he had dismounted to drink at the spring, and his horse,
terrified by the grizzly, had bolted. " We tried
to put him on a horse," said Bridger, " but he
screamed, though he didn't seem to know nothing;
and so Fitz said he'd stay with the old man while
I came back."

It was, of course, impractical to move the whole
party on to the forks at that late hour, so the
Major sent two men back with Bridger to watch
over old Glass until the main body should come
up next day. It was commonly believed in camp
that night that the old man was " done for "; but
when the party arrived at the forks next morning,
he was still living though he had not regained
consciousness. What should be done? As
Bridger had stated, it was impossible to move
him; and certainly the whole expedition could not
be delayed indefinitely while one man decided
whether or not he was going to die. Finally two
men were induced, by the offer of a liberal reward,
to remain with the wounded man until he could
be placed either on a horse or under the ground.
Then the main body, impatient at the delay, be-

cause the way before them was long and the scarcity of horses made their progress slow, struck out for the Yellowstone over practically the same route that Jed and Baptiste had taken in June.[1]

Ill luck still followed Henry. Scarcely had the party crossed the desolate country through which the upper waters of the Little Missouri run, and entered the valley of the Yellowstone, when a large war party of Indians, thought to be Gros Ventres, swooped down upon it. During the brisk fight that followed, four trappers were killed and several more horses were wounded.

During the evening of the day after the battle, the two men who had been left to watch over old Glass at the forks of the Grand, rode their fagged horses into camp, and the saddle of the horse they led was empty. Few words were expected from them by their comrades. They said that they had remained at the forks four days; then old Hugh had " gone under " and had been decently buried. They had brought all his " fixins " away with them, including gun, blanket, powder-horn, knife, and flint and steel. The story they brought occasioned no surprise, and little sorrow was directly expressed, though many spoke kindly of the dead that night, remembering much good of the

[1] The Missouri *Intelligencer,* June 18, 1825; Sage's "Scenes in the Rocky Mountains"; Ruxton's "Adventures in Mexico"; Howe's "Hist. Collections of the Great West"; Cooke's "Scenes in the U. S. Army."

graybearded old hunter — how cool he had been in the Ree fight, the droll things he had said on such and such occasions, feats of strength he had performed when a keelboat had grounded on a bar, and many lesser matters such as make men love men.

Well, the old fellow was " rubbed out " at last, but it took a grizzly bear to do the job, and that was something. It would have been worth a year's wages to see that bear-fight! So it was. You never knew when your time might come. Thereupon the camp slept.

Pushing on down the Yellowstone without meeting any further resistance, Henry arrived at his post to find that, during his absence, the Blackfeet and Assiniboines had driven off twenty-two of the horses he had left there. Within a few days after his arrival seven more were stolen by the Assiniboines. Obviously, the chances for successful operations in that vicinity were slight. So the Major decided to abandon the post and move back up the Yellowstone into the country of the Crows who, owing to the hostility existing between them and the Blackfeet, generally welcomed the trappers, not only as allies against their ancient foes, but also as a ready source of ammunition. Furthermore, the presence of Edward Rose, who, as has been noted, had won a high place in the tribe, would doubtless do much to insure a friendly reception for the hitherto luckless band.

It will be remembered that twenty men were

left in charge of the fort when Henry descended the Missouri to reinforce Ashley's party below the Ree towns. Having set out from the mouth of the Grand with eighty men, and having lost seven on the way, he now had ninety-three under his command — a formidable party, sadly hampered, however, by the insufficient number of its horses. Heartened by this new hope of a peaceful winter among a friendly people, the trappers marched southwestward up the valley of the Yellowstone for several days. Already there had been heavy night-frosts, and flocks of blackbirds, brawling in the thickets, proclaimed the coming of the winter. They were travelling now through a region of ready feasts. Bison and deer and antelope were plentiful; and often, topping a rise for a long gaze, they saw great herds of what seemed at first to be mules, and were elk. Every evening the hunters came in with goodly horse-loads of fresh meat, so that there was singing as the sun went down, and in the warmth and glow of the embers the men remembered many tales.

Then one day it seemed that bad luck, like a huge cat, had only been playing with them, allowing a brief respite from care that the next pounce might be crushing. Toward evening the advance guard came galloping back to report a large war party of Indians some two or three miles ahead. Grumbling and sullen, the trappers began to prepare for another battle, unsaddling the pack ani-

mals and making a breastwork of the baggage.
While they were thus engaged, three Indian horsemen suddenly appeared on a bluff-top several hundred yards away. They were making signs of
peace, and Rose, believing them to be Crows,
mounted and rode toward them. After having
covered half the distance to the bluff, he paused to
exchange signs with the three strangers, then,
pricking his horse, he hastened to join those on the
bluff-top. Anxiously the camp watched the panto-
mime on the height where an animated confab was
evidently in progress; and there were many who
questioned the loyalty of the ex-pirate. Might
he not betray them to his adopted people that he
might win more prestige with the tribe? However, Henry, who had known the man in the early
days of the Missouri Fur Company, had no such
fears.

Rose galloped back at length, bringing the best
of news. The three on the bluff had proven to
be old friends of his, members of a Crow war
party returning with many horses from a foray
into the Blackfoot country. They welcomed the
whites into their land, and wished nothing better
than to trade, for they were in need of many
things, especially powder and ball with which to
meet their enemies on the north.

When the Crows came up and went into camp
a short distance away, that which had been reported as a large war party was seen to consist

of no more than twenty five braves, but the horses they drove were many. The night was given over to feasting and trade; and, through old Rose as interpreter, the trappers and Indians exchanged tales of prowess, backed upon both sides by an eloquent display of scalps — Blackfoot, Gros Ventre, Ree! Had the white men fought, and did they hate the Blackfeet with a big hate? It was enough. The Crows would be friends forever!

In the morning when the two parties took up the march again, both were richer and happier than on the day before, though their combined wealth was no greater; for the Indians might now meet their foes with plenty of powder, and the trappers, with all the horses they could use, were entering a friendly country rich in beaver.

IX

JED WRESTLES WITH DEATH

IT was now time for the fall hunt to begin, and
accordingly it was decided that a small party
should strike southward along the eastern border
of the Crow country, locating the richest beaver
streams and trapping on the way, while the main
body should move on up the Yellowstone to the
mouth of the Big Horn, there to establish winter
quarters.   At the mouth of the Powder sixteen
men were told off for this undertaking, William
L. Sublette being one of the number.   Jed Smith
and Thomas Fitzpatrick were placed in command.

Bidding farewell to their comrades, these
pushed southward up the valley of the Powder.
Beaver sign was fairly plentiful.   Traps set in the
evening generally yielded satisfactory returns in
the morning; and the better part of each afternoon was spent in skinning the catch and preparing the pelts.   Travelling leisurely thus through
a region where fresh meat could be procured with
little difficulty, the men worked contentedly toward the Big Horn Mountains that at length began to lift clearer and clearer in the southwest.
Here indeed was life such as these young fellows

had dreamed of in the humdrum of the settlements. Autumn brooded goldenly on the vast land of no restraint. How glorious to be young and free!

For a week the party kept together; then Smith, with five men, struck out westward. Fitzpatrick, with the balance of the trappers, kept on up the valley, hoping to fall in with the Crow nation then on its fall buffalo hunt in the region between the headwaters of the Powder and the North Fork of the Platte. Smith was to explore the country westward, trapping on the upper reaches of the Tongue and Rosebud as he went, and meet Fitzpatrick returning by way of the Big Horn, whence the reunited bands should proceed to winter quarters on the Yellowstone.

For several days Smith and his men worked slowly up a small tributary stream that came down from the divide between the Powder and the Tongue, and the hunting was good. Then one evening Jed met with an accident that seemed likely to end his dream of the great mysterious white spaces beyond the Rockies. He had been setting a trap at the margin of the creek and was pushing up through the brush that fringed the bank, when a huge hairy form towered growling above him.

There followed a period of torturing dreams; and when he awoke it was night and he was lying beside a fire with his shadowy comrades leaning

over him.   There was a roaring ache in his head,
and at intervals a stabbing pain shot through one
of his hips.   He had been felled with a blow
from the paw of a grizzly, his thigh had been
badly mangled, and he was in a fair way to be
rubbed out when his comrades, who were setting
traps in the vicinity, had rushed to his rescue and
killed the bear.

As in the case of old Hugh Glass, it was plain
enough that Jed, though conscious, would be unable to travel for many days; and that night it
was decided that three of the party should go in
pursuit of Fitzpatrick, the two others remaining
to watch over the wounded man.   For several
days after the departure of the three, things went
well enough in the camp by the nameless creek;
and though it was evident that Jed's recovery
would be slow, and though signs of approaching
winter were not lacking, there seemed to be little
reason for uneasiness.   The Rees and Blackfeet
were far away, and the Gros Ventres were doubtless hunting buffalo on the plains bordering the
Missouri.   Deer and antelope abounded in the
broken country round about; so there would be
no lack of fresh meat, and Jed's companions
could profitably spend the time of waiting in collecting beaver pelts.

But one evening, a half hour or so after the
two men had gone up-stream to set their traps,
leaving their horses staked near the camp, Jed

heard a number of shots, fired in rapid succession, and a medley of wild cries. The sounds came from the direction in which his comrades had gone. Considering the number of shots and voices, there was but one conclusion to draw. Seizing his rifle and powder-horn, Jed, at the cost of excruciating pain, dragged himself into the midst of a thicket nearby and waited breathlessly. Very soon there was a crashing of the brush up-stream, and a dozen Indians in war paint came cantering down the creek. Catching sight of the camp and the three grazing horses, the band halted, dismounted, and, gabbling excitedly in a tongue that Jed did not recognize, proceeded to appropriate the animals and whatever articles of equipment that struck their fancy.

During this time several were poking about in the brush with the muzzles of their guns, and Jed had decided that his last hour on earth was about to end, when, at a command from one of the party, they all leaped upon their horses and galloped off down stream. But during the few moments when the camp was being looted, the wounded man in the brush had seen that which told a tragic story — two dripping scalps, the hair of which he recognized only too well!

The dusk fell with a penetrating chill and the long and terrible night began. Jed crawled out of his hiding place, and after much patient industry, accompanied by torture, he managed to gather together a small heap of dry twigs.   But though he had a flint and steel he struck no fire, lest the Indians, camping in the vicinity, might return. The blankets had gone with the rest of the equipment, and there in that chill immensity the sick man shivered, thinking of his dead comrades and haunted with the most gloomy forebodings. Would Fitzpatrick return that way before it was too late?   How many days would it take to die of starvation?   How many nights like this could one endure?   Why endure the cold any longer? Why fear sudden death at the hands of savages, with that slow death waiting at the end of many days and nights of suffering?

By and by in the wee hours of the morning he made a fire, and heartened by its cheerful glow and warmth, he thanked God that, for all his woe, he had not only his rifle, knife, and flint and steel, but, what was more, the much worn copy of the Bible which he always carried in a pocket of his hunting shirt — a practice which had occasioned considerable sly merriment among his less pious comrades.

For awhile now he strove to read by the dancing light, and his memory supplied what he could not follow with his eyes.   " He is chastened also with pain upon his bed, and the multitude of his bones with strong pain. . . . Yea, his soul draweth near to the grave, and his life to the destroyers. . . . His flesh shall be fresher than a child's; he shall return to the days of his youth. He shall pray unto God and He will be favorable unto him. . . ."

Jed fell into an uneasy sleep. When he awoke, the fire was out, but the dawn had come. In the new light the old sustaining faith came on him like a revelation. God was in the world as much as ever, and He would provide. Yonder ran pure water — a tremendous blessing. As for food, doubtless his comrades had set traps nearby, and there is much poorer food than beaver flesh.

Having prayed earnestly for strength to endure the pain he was about to suffer, he dragged himself along the bank, keeping a sharp lookout for traps. The first was empty, and the second also. Appalled at the pain that his venture was costing him, he lay still for some time, nursing the forebodings of the night. But at length prayer strengthened him, and he began to drag himself again. The third trap contained a beaver; but it was an hour before Jed succeeded in bringing it ashore by means of a forked branch cut from the brush.

It was nearly noon when he finished his breakfast; and for hours he lay exhausted, dreading the passing of the day. Then at length, when the sun was nearing the western horizon, he began to collect fuel for the night.

The next day he fasted, for he found no beaver; and still another day came and went without food. Game seemed suddenly to have deserted the re-

gion, that his trial might be the greater. He
turned to the Book for courage. "I will lift up
mine eyes unto the hills, from whence cometh my
help. My help cometh from the Lord which
made heaven and earth. . . . The Lord shall preserve thee from evil. . . ."

In the early morning of the third day of fast-
ing Jed's prayers were answered. He wakened
suddenly, rubbed his eyes, and saw a buck deer
drinking at the stream an easy rifle-shot away.
Without lifting his head he reached for the loaded
gun that lay beside him, and turning on his side,
took careful aim just behind the shoulder of the
buck. At the roar of the gun it went down,
floundering in the mud, and then was still.

Praising the goodness of God, he feasted that
day; and having feasted, he dragged himself up
the torturing slope of a nearby hillock, and lying
there, he searched the empty distances all day
long. Nothing appeared but a flock of crows.

But answered prayer had enormously strengthened the old faith in him. What if Fitzpatrick
did not return? No man who knows God can
be alone, and a way would be made. Doubtless
his hip would heal enough before the winter set
in so that he might make his way alone to the
mouth of the Big Horn.

For three days he fed from the flesh of the
buck, keeping constant watch over a flock of crows
that were bent upon robbing his larder, and fright-

ening them away whenever they swooped down. Then what remained of the meat went putrid, and the crows, in a noisy black cloud, soon stripped the bones clean. Jed watched them and wondered how long it would be before they should be feasting on human flesh.

He spent the two following days upon the hillock without food. Once a herd of antelope appeared a half mile away. For hours they remained in sight, peacefully grazing; then they disappeared. The third day after his meat supply had failed, he did not attempt to climb out of the creek bottom, and somehow his prayers seemed feeble. He thought much now of the home folks back in Ashtabula, Ohio, and there were times when he visualized them all with a startling clearness. Would he ever see them with his eyes again?

"The Lord is my shepherd," he read; "I shall not want. He maketh me to lie down in green pastures; he leadeth me beside the still waters. Yea, though I walk through the valley of the shadow of death, I will fear no evil; for Thou art with me." These words, oft repeated, added power to his prayers; and during the fourth day after the crows had picked the carcass, God seemed to hear again, for three deer came down to the creek to drink some two hundred yards away. But when Jed took aim, the mark danced about giddily. He fired. A jet of water arose

ten yards short of the drinking animals, that
crashed through the brush and disappeared.   He
turned to the Book for strength with which to
bear this disappointment.   " Thou preparest a
table before me in the presence of mine enemies. . . ."

Was he being mocked?   What had he done
that the Almighty should desert him?   Earnestly
now he implored forgiveness for his sins that he
might die in peace; and a soothing quiet came
upon him.

The next day Colonel Keemle of the Missouri
Fur Company, led by the three who had gone in
search of Fitzpatrick, came riding up the creek
with a band of trappers.   These were the survivors of the Blackfoot disaster on Pryor's Fork
of the Yellowstone during the previous spring,
when Jones and Immel had been slain.

By securing a blanket across two poles, the ends
of which were fastened to the pack saddles of two
of the more docile horses, a litter was made for
Jed, whose wounds, despite his lack of food, had
healed sufficiently to admit of travel.   Pushing
westward across the upper waters of the Tongue,
Keemle's party came to the camp of a roving band
of Cheyennes, and there, in a few days, came Fitzpatrick and his men.   They had met and travelled
for some days with the Crows who would soon
return to the mouth of the Big Horn for the
winter.

Fitzpatrick had conceived a big idea during his absence; and, riding beside the horse-litter as the party travelled down the valley of the Little Big Horn toward winter quarters, he and Jed eagerly discussed plans for a spring expedition. A Crow chief had told how, following up the Sweetwater, which flows into the North Fork of the Platte, one would come to a break in the Wind River Mountains through which one might travel as easily as over open prairie down to the Siskadee Agie,[1] as the Indians called Green River. So plentiful were the beaver yonder, the Crow chief had said, that traps were not needed; one could knock over all one wanted with a club![2]

How this story must have fired the imagination of the wounded man! Here, at last, was news from the mysterious white spaces! The gates to the world of his dream were about to swing wide!

A keen northwind was bringing the winter when they reached the Yellowstone. There near the mouth of the Big Horn, and not far from the abandoned post that Manuel Lisa had built sixteen years before, snug winter quarters had been erected by Henry's men. Shortly after the arrival of Smith and Fitzpatrick, a party that had been sent northwest into the country of the Blackfeet returned with more thrilling tales than beaver.

Thus united again, Henry's men settled down

[1] Meaning "Sage Hen River."
[2] Article by "Solitaire" in *St. Louis Weekly Reveille*, March 1st, 1847.

for the winter, trapping the streams of the region and trading with the Crows, who had come up from the south and pitched their skin lodges nearby.

X

THE GHOST

THE new year, 1824, arrived in the midst of tremendous blizzards, and for weeks the trappers had nothing to do but to eat, sleep, sing, clog to a *voyageur's* fiddling, and to swap yarns. The latter occupation offered the best avenue of escape from tedium; for man is so constituted that he is never really happy except when creative, and yarning, as these men understood it, was, at its best, certainly much more than a memory exercise! The craving for sensation during those shut-in days and nights, together with the keen spirit of rivalry that grew up among the story-tellers, often spurred them on to splendid mendacities. The old veteran from the Southwest was perhaps the most successful practitioner of this primitive art, owing partly, no doubt, to a native talent for being quite unashamed, and partly to the fact that his alleged adventures were sufficiently remote both in time and space to give his imagination the proper focal length for seeing large.

Was there anyone present who had never heard

of that terrible beast called the carcagne? [1] Well, the old veteran from the Southwest had seen one with his own eyes, and could describe it in every particular.   Not only had he seen one, but once when he and a companion were roasting a goat away down yonder near the Spanish Peaks, a carcagne had come bounding into camp, seized the meat from the fire and disappeared — all with incredible speed.   With every question from his audience, the old man's memory seemed to grow richer, until the original version of the incident was no more than the simple musical theme which the winds and strings and brasses chase wildly through the intricate mazes of an involved orchestration.   And what was the carcagne like? Well, its hair was long, coarse, and black, and had the peculiar property of growing longer, coarser, and blacker upon closer scrutiny.   As to general appearance, this strange beast was a perfect wolf from the tip of its nose to its shoulders, and thereafter it was a bear, though it was far bigger than any bear the deponent had ever seen. Its cry was indescribable, and was such as to strike terror into the stoutest heart.

However, marvelous as the carcagne, upon repeated examination, proved to be, the telling of this tale was the merest preliminary exercise for

---

[1] In his "Rocky Mountain Life," published in 1857, Rufus B. Sage seriously discussed this mythical monster that had then existed in the imagination of the trappers for a generation.

the old veteran. His memory became more athletic, and he recalled the Munchies.[1] And what were the Munchies? Why, they were a tribe of white Indians — whiter than Americans — living away down yonder beyond the Gila country. The old veteran had met a man who had seen the Munchies; in fact, the old veteran had seen them with his own eyes. He had not only seen them; he had lived in one of their huge cities for some months, and he could testify to the fact that they were a highly civilized people.

It happened in this way. Perhaps the youngsters present hadn't heard of McKnight, Baird and Chambers; but doubtless the older men would remember how those gentlemen had set out from St. Louis on a trading expedition to Santa Fé in the spring of 1812. Well, anyway, the speaker had been induced by those gentlemen to accompany the party as hunter, his great skill in that line having already rendered him famous, as one might say. Upon entering the Mexican country, the party, consisting of twelve men, was seized by the Spanish authorities and sent to prison in Chihuahua, there to remain until death, it would appear. But the speaker, being an exceedingly clever man, had contrived to escape — in three or four distinct ways, as the highly circumstantial

[1] Another myth current in the Early West. See Sage's " Rocky Mountain Life," Chapter XXIV.

narrative seemed to indicate.   Once outside the
prison, the hero of his own story fled to the mountains to evade his pursuers.

For weeks he wandered about, lost in the
wilderness of mountains; and, having no weapon,
it began to appear that he would surely die of
starvation.   Then, one day, summoning all his
power in a last desperate effort, he climbed to the
top of a very high mountain.   And what did his
hearers suppose he saw?

The old veteran was a master of dramatic
pauses, which served, doubtless, the double purpose of intensifying the interest of his audience
and giving the narrator an opportunity to recall
any episode that, owing to the well-known care-
lessness of Chance, might have failed to happen.

Well, on its further side, that mountain range
dropped sheer a thousand feet or more to a fertile
cup-like valley apparently hemmed in on all sides
by a giddy precipice.   And lo, spread out on the
valley floor was a vast city with spires and domes
that shone in the sun!   Yonder was food at last
— but how to reach it?   All the rest of that day
the narrator of the tale sought in vain for a means
of descent; and next day he continued his search,
until in mid-afternoon he came to a ragged fissure
in the cliff, down which, by dint of native clever-
ness and prodigious strength, he managed to make
his way.   He found the plain to be far vaster in
extent than he had supposed (and the city itself

proportionately larger), so that it was not until the next morning that he reached his destination, though he continued to travel most of the night.

The Munchies (for it was their city that had been seen from the top of the mountain) appeared to be unaware that any other human beings existed, and they received the starved trapper as a god. Processions and feasts were the order of the day. Housed in a huge temple, where he was daily adored by thousands, the old trapper grew fat and dissatisfied. Had he only been treated as a human being, he might have been there yet, the contented father of a brood of Munchies. But being a god soon wearied him, and he began to yearn for the old free life. Accordingly, one dark night, he made his escape, reaching the fissure in the cliff just at the white of dawn. He climbed all that day, and when, at sunset, he stood on the crest of the mountain, he could see the whole Munchie population rushing wildly about the plain like a colony of agitated ants.

The narrator had, at the time, intended to return; not alone, to be sure, but with a dozen hardy fellows properly armed. The Munchies were rich beyond calculation, even the poorest citizens eating from plates of solid gold. Furthermore, being vegetarians, because there were no wild animals in their valley, and having no word for " enemy " in their vocabulary, they were without weapons of any sort.

The business possibilities there were certainly very inviting!

And why hadn't the old veteran gone back? Well, he had tried to go back two years later, and a score of others with him. For months he and his companions had climbed lofty peaks, looking for the city of the Munchies, but in vain.

Who were the Munchies and whence came they? That was indeed a puzzling matter; but the narrator, having brought a Munchie coin away with him, once showed the same to a priest who declared that the inscription thereon was in the best Latin. Doubtless the Munchies were descendants of a small band of Roman adventurers who, having crossed the Atlantic something like 1,500 years before Columbus, had been lost in the wilderness!

The coin? The old veteran regretted exceedingly to report that he had lost the coin some years back under circumstances involving a clash with hostile Indians — which reminded him of another story well calculated to discourage any further questioning with reference to the mysterious city, lost forever in the wilds of Chihuahua.

So, mounting to the greater audacity by way of the lesser, the old veteran often reached dizzy pinnacles of improvisation, entertaining himself quite as much as his comrades. But there is in this cosmos of ours a story-making agency that at times, though working only in the raw stuff of

facts, outdoes man's boldest fictions. That
agency is generally known as Chance. The least
sensitive prevaricator feels it incumbent upon
himself to give even his wildest yarns some
semblance of plausibility, which is a matter of
logical sequences. But Chance, being unhuman,
is under no compulsion to be plausible, and is apparently subject only to that weird super-logic of
events, the course of which is non-predictable by
any mental process. A story thus created does
not woo credence step by step; it simply over-
whelms incredulity with the impossible accomplished, and leaves the critic grasping the broken
chain of his logic.

Now a masterpiece of this order had been in
preparation ever since the westbound party had
passed the forks of the Grand River during the
previous August; and so audaciously improbable
was the tale, that had it been told by the old veteran of the Southwest, it would probably have
been received with hilarious laughter, for all the
sadness of it.

It happened thus. The blizzards that had
ushered in the new year, 1824, had ceased at last,
and a great white calm had fallen on the wilderness. It was now nearly February. The men
were beginning to look forward to the renewed
activity of the spring hunt, and Fitzpatrick's
plans for pushing westward through the pass, of
which the Crows had told him, into the mysteri-

ous beaver country whence all streams sought the Pacific, furnished an enthralling topic for conversation. Even the Crows had not penetrated far into the region now about to be visited. It seemed somewhat like planning a trip to the other side of the moon.

Night had fallen, and the hush of intense cold was upon the white waste. A merry fire roared on the hearth in the big trading room where the men were lounging. Old Baptiste was making the Major's fiddle laugh and weep, and often when his bow swung into some old Southern jig tune, the younger fellows would step it lively, aping the Negro dancers away down yonder on the plantations that used to be home. By and by, in a momentary hush, the stockade gate was heard to rattle at its bar as though a sudden wind had shaken it; yet there was no wind. The men listened awhile, but heard only the howling of the wolves and the fort timbers popping in the great freeze.

The music began again, and a youth, swinging into an extravagant Negro clog, aroused a roar of laughter. Again the music stopped; and scarcely had the silence returned, when a wild hoarse cry arose outside. Some Crow Indian was there at the gate, no doubt; but what could he want? A trapper got up, went out into the snow that whined under his moccasins, and, followed by the candle-glimmer that spilled through the open door, went to the gate and raised the wicket through which trading was sometimes carried on. Immediately those inside heard the wicket clatter down, and with a look of terror on his face the trapper dashed back into the room and slammed the door.

"I — I — saw —" he stammered.

"Saw what?" asked the Major.

"Old Glass!" whispered the trapper "—all. white — his ghost!"

"Fiddlesticks!" said the Major. Getting up from his bench by the fire, he went out into the starlit silence, and the men thronged to the door. The dry snow fifed to his stride. The chain clanked; the gate swung wide. And then the impossible came to pass! The men saw Henry walking backward, and after him came no other than Hugh Glass who had died yonder at the forks of the Grand and was buried there! His hair that swept his shoulders and his long gray beard matted upon his chest were ghostly with his frozen breath. The men gave way at the door, and Henry backed in, followed by the spectre. And what a face it had — grotesquely blurred as though seen reflected in ruffled water!

The old man stalked boldly into the middle of the room with his long rifle under his arm and stared about him.

"My God!" gasped the Major; "two men saw you die at the forks of the Grand!"

The old man's chest rumbled with unpleasant laughter.

"Show me these men who have seen so much," he said. "Either they lie here or I lie there! I'm not half sure myself."

"Yonder is one," said Henry.

Hugh turned to where a trapper crouched against the wall with abject terror in his eyes. For a brief moment the ruined face of the old man was as though a blizzard swept across it. He set the trigger of his gun and clicked the lock. Then his face softened, and, easing the hammer down, he strode over to the grovelling man and kicked him lightly.

"Get up and wag your tail," said he; "I wouldn't kill a pup. Where's the other one who saw me die?"

The other one had gone to Fort Atkinson with despatches before the snows had come; and the other one proved to be a youth whom Hugh had loved and befriended.

"Well, well," remarked the man who had just returned from the grave; "it's a long way I've travelled if yonder gentleman has spoken truth. So put on the pot and you will see what an appetite a ghost can have!" And having eaten with a wolfish hunger, the old man told the story of his resurrection.

He could not say how long he had lain there by the spring; but by and by he awoke and managed to get his eyes open. It was some time before he could realize what had happened to him. Then he knew by the footprints of horses all about him that the main party had been there and gone on. The ash-heap of an old fire, however, showed that Major Henry had not intended to desert him. Some of his comrades had been left behind to care for him; but where were they? And where were his "fixins"? Not even so much as a knife had been left him.

The more he thought about the matter the greater grew his anger, and he swore that he would live that he might avenge that treachery. Deliberately he set about the difficult business of getting well enough to travel. The spring furnished plenty of good water, and over it hung a bush full of ripe bullberries. Also, with his teeth he was able to tear flesh from the gashed body of the bear; but the meat had begun to spoil, and soon he had only the fruit and what bread-root he could find in the vicinity.

After some days of waiting he decided that his leg, which seemed to have been broken, was hardly likely to carry him for some weeks; so he thought it well to begin his journey at once by crawling. Fort Kiowa, the nearest post on the Missouri, was over a hundred miles away. After weeks of well nigh incredible hardships, sorely wounded and without weapons, he had succeeded in reaching the post. Shortly afterward, still intent upon revenge, he had joined a keelboat party bound for the mouth of the Yellowstone; but at the Mandan villages the ice had closed in. Still driven by his wrath, he had pushed on alone through the winter wilderness; and here he was at the mouth of the Big Horn!

The wrath that had given him strength to survive was now concentrated upon the friend who had robbed and deserted him; and within a few weeks he set out again, riding southward by way of the Powder to the Platte, eastward to the Niobrara, down that stream to its mouth, and thence by the valley of the Missouri to Fort Atkinson. But the treacherous friend had gone up stream, and Hugh followed.

If, when the long pursuit was ended, Hugh had wrought vengeance upon his youthful betrayer, his adventure would have been little more than an astonishing exhibition of brute endurance and ferocity; but in the end the Graybeard forgave, and that fact raises his story to the level of sublimity.[1]

[1] A detailed account of the adventure will be found in my narrative poem, "The Song of Hugh Glass," Macmillan, 1915; annotated school edition, 1919.

XI

THE FIRST WHITE MEN THROUGH SOUTH PASS

LATE in February of 1824 the monotonous days of the winter-bound party at the mouth of the Big Horn came to an end at last. A small band of trappers, including Hugh Glass, still obsessed with the desire for revenge, started with despatches for Fort Atkinson, and those who remained soon after began the spring hunt, trapping on the tributaries of the Yellowstone in the vicinity of the fort.

Meanwhile, waiting for the first authentic signs of spring, Thomas Fitzpatrick and Jedediah Smith were making ready for the much discussed journey across the Great Divide into the mysterious beaver country of which the Crows had given so glowing an account during the previous fall. It was agreed with the Major that they should undertake this expedition as " free trappers," the necessary outfit to be furnished on credit by the firm of Ashley and Henry, and to be paid for out of the proceeds of the enterprise — a fact which made the young adventurers all the more eager to put their fortune to the test.

The snow was softening in a southwind, and up

the lower reaches of the sunward slopes a pale
green glow was filtering through the yellow buffalo grass the day they rode away from the fort
and disappeared up the valley of the Big Horn.
It must have been good to see them riding forth
that day — a score of hardy young men, wearing
the savage garb of the wilderness, well mounted,
and driving with them a string of laden pack-
horses.

Day after day they pushed on steadily up the
valley, making but moderate progress; for the
winter had been a hard one and forage for the
horses had been scanty in the vicinity of the fort.
Nor did they seem to be riding toward the spring,
though they were headed that way; for the land
was rising rapidly and the increasing altitude off-
set their southward progress, so that the ponies,
nosing for the first green shoots, still tasted snow.
To their left and ahead arose the dazzling sum-
mits of the Big Horn Mountains, and to their
right the Continental Divide was like an irregular
bank of glittering cloud floating up with an im-
perceptible westwind.

They came at length to the base of the mountains where the Big Horn River issues from a
canyon, and began the crossing of the range by a
route that came to be known among the trappers
as " Bad Pass," and that was described by Irving (who got his information from Captain Bonneville) as " rugged and frightful."   At this early

season the passage must have been especially difficult, and doubtless two or three days were spent in crossing, though the length of the canyon by which the river breaks through is only thirty miles.

Upon emerging from the mountains they found themselves in the pleasant valley of the Wind River which, rising in the Wind River Mountains, flows southeastward then northward, and after breaking through the range that had just been crossed becomes the Big Horn. Here on the 9th of September, thirteen years before, had arrived the Astorians under W. P. Hunt, travelling overland from the Ree villages on the Missouri to the mouth of the Columbia. From this point Hunt's trail had led up the Wind River through a difficult pass near Jackson's Hole. But according to the information that Fitzpatrick had received from the Crows, he should here strike southward to the Sweetwater which, if followed to its source, would lead to the easy open gateway of a country rich in beaver.

During the ascent of the Big Horn and the crossing of the mountains it had become evident that at least half of the horses were too poor to be relied upon for any difficult going that might be encountered farther on; and it was decided that a half dozen men under Smith, who no doubt still felt the effects of his wounds, should remain for a time on the Wind River with the weaker horses, later crossing with them to the Sweetwater, there

to await the exploring party's return from the
West during the summer.

Accordingly, near the mouth of the Popo Agie,
a tributary of the Wind River, Smith went into
camp, and Fitzpatrick with fourteen men and
about twenty-five of the stronger horses pushed on
southward up the valley of the little tributary.
Very soon after leaving Smith, the wisdom of the
late decision became apparent to Fitzpatrick, for
he found himself in a " confusion of hills and cliffs
of red sandstone, some peaked and angular, some
round, some broken into crags and precipices, and
piled up in fantastic masses; but all naked and
sterile." [1]   Emerging from this grotesque world
and travelling as rapidly as possible through a
broken sagebrush country where the banks of the
creeks were often crusted white with saline deposits, they came at last, with horses half starved
and fagged, to a clear pure stream flowing swiftly
eastward over a rocky bed through a fine valley
dotted here and there with clumps of cottonwood,
scrub oak, and aspen.   It was the Sweetwater, the
origin of whose name would seem to be obvious,
considering the purity of the stream as contrasted
with the saline character of the creeks in the surrounding region.[2]   Wherever the snow, swept

---

[1] Irving, Captain Bonneville.
[2] The original French name was *Eau Sucrée* (sugared water),
and W. A. Ferris, an early traveller over the Oregon Trail,
tells us that the name was given because a pack-mule, laden
with sugar, had been lost in the river sometime before 1830.

thin by the winds, had begun to melt in the noon suns, a rich growth of buffalo grass, well cured during the winter, furnished excellent pasturage; and the party spent several days in camp here, that the animals might recruit their strength for the journey across the Great Divide.

To westward the Wind River Mountains ran like a broken white wall along the horizon, and the men, remembering their recent experiences in the Big Horn range, talked much of the difficulties that might be encountered yonder at this time of the year, for the snow would still be lying deep in the lofty passes. Would it not be better to wait until the spring thaw had cleared the way? But Fitzpatrick, eager to enter the promised land of which the Crows had spoken, and trusting in what the Chief had told him as to the ease with which the mountains could be crossed, chose to push on without further delay. Setting out up the valley of the Sweetwater, they travelled all day over a natural road, no portion of which would have offered any serious obstacle to loaded wagons. Sometimes the valley spread to a width of three or four miles, sometimes it narrowed to a few rods, but always the way was fairly easy; and the rise of the land toward the Divide was scarcely perceptible, save that the air grew steadily colder and the snow deepened as the party proceeded. That night the sky was like frosty steel and the stars like broken glass.

Breaking camp in the white of the dawn, they pushed on again; and more and more, as they went, their horses floundered in the crusted snow. The Sweetwater dwindled to a little creek voiceless in the grip of the winter that lingered there, and the noon was like a mid-winter noon. They toiled on over a high rolling prairie, the ponies frosty-muzzled and frosty-flanked, the men's beards whitened with their breath. By and by the Sweetwater had disappeared. For some time the band toiled on silently, save for the blowing of the horses and the crunching of the crusted snow. Then someone cried: " Look! Look! "

Long vistas of a vast undulating plain had opened out ahead, and here and there in the distance lofty buttes (some flat-topped like islands deserted by the sea, some carved by wind and rain into towers and domes) seemed staring round them at the immense scope and loneliness of the surrounding world. It was the promised land of the Siskadee Agie, and already they were on the westward slope of the Divide. The shout that arose from the band died without echo in that vastness, and the sympathetic neighing of the horses was a feeble sound.

Now as they floundered on they noted that the air grew somewhat warmer, despite the waning of the afternoon. Signs of noonday melting began to appear. Shortly before sundown they came upon a living spring, where they went into camp and spent a cheerless night, for there was no wood in the vicinity; but the windswept spaces about the spring furnished some scanty grazing for the horses, which was the matter of chief importance.

All the next forenoon, as they pushed on in a southwesterly direction, signs of spring became increasingly evident. Yesterday morning it was January; today it was late March. The grass had begun to sprout and the willow buds were swelling slightly when they came, in the late afternoon, to a creek the bed of which was some fifteen or twenty feet wide. They were now on the Little Sandy, the waters of which reach the Gulf of California by way of the Colorado; and they had just come through South Pass — the first white men of all the thousands upon thousands that would pass that way when the Oregon and California Trail should become like a great river of home-seeking humanity.[1]

That night by a cheerful fire, Fitzpatrick indulged in what must have seemed extravagant prophecy to many of his companions, telling how ox-drawn wagons would one day be seen trundling up the valleys of the Platte and the Sweetwater to this place, thence to the headwaters of the Co-

[1] See article entitled "Major Fitzpatrick, Discoverer of South Pass," by Solitaire (John S. Robb) in *St. Louis Weekly Reveille,* March 1, 1847; article entitled "The Plains" by François des Montagnes in *Western Journal,* St. Louis, 1852, Vol. IX; H. C. Dale's article, "Did the Returning Astorians Discover South Pass?" in Oregon Historical Society Quarterly, Vol. XVII; H. C. Dale, "Ashley-Smith Explorations," page 93 et seq.

lumbia and down that river to the sea. "Little
did he dream then," says an old chronicler, "that
he himself, twenty years after, would encamp in
that passage with the first train of American emi-
grants destined to the new land beyond, and who
were not only carrying along their wagons, but all
the household necessaries for furnishing their new
homes." [1]

[1] *St. Louis Reveille,* March 1, 1847.

XII

TREASURE AND TROUBLE THEREWITH

MOVING on down the creek to its junction with the Big Sandy,[1] and following the latter to its mouth through an arid country, Fitzpatrick's party and the full tide of spring reached the Green River together. The long-leafed cottonwoods and the box elders that grew along the river banks and on occasional islands were leafing out, and late April was moving like a pale green vapor through the willow thickets. Food for man and beast was plentiful here. But the beaver! Everywhere felled cottonwoods, dams, and dome-shaped lodges proclaimed the wealth of the country; and the men set to work in high glee, for none among them had ever before seen a country so rich in fur. Certainly the Crow chief had not been over-eloquent in his description of this paradise of the trapper!

Joseph Meek, a famous mountain man, has left us the following account of the manner in which the trapper took his game:[2] "He has an or-

[1] This stream was named by Ashley in April, 1825. See Chap. XIV.

[2] Victor. "River of the West."

dinary steel trap weighing five pounds, attached to
a chain five feet long, with a swivel and ring at
the end, which plays round what is called the float,
a dry stick of wood about six feet long. The
trapper wades out into the stream, which is shallow, and cuts with his knife a bed for his trap, five
or six inches under water. He then takes the
float out the whole length of the chain in the direction of the center of the stream, and drives it in,
so fast that the beaver can not draw it out; at the
same time tying the other end by a thong to the
bank. A small stick or twig, dipped in musk or
castor (found in certain glands of the beaver)
served for bait, and is placed so as to hang directly
above the trap, which is now set. The trapper
then throws water plentifully over the adjacent
bank to conceal any footprints or scent by which
the beaver would be alarmed, and, going to some
distance, wades out of the stream. In setting a
trap, certain things are to be observed with care;
first, that the trap is firmly fixed, and at the proper
distance from the bank — for if the beaver can
get on shore with the trap, he will cut off his foot
to escape; second, that the float is of dry wood,
for should it not be, the animal will cut it off at a
stroke, and swimming with the trap to the middle
of the dam, be drowned by its weight. In the latter case, when the hunter visits his trap in the
morning, he is under the necessity of plunging into
the water and swimming out, to dive for his game.

Should the morning be frosty and chilly, as it very frequently is in the mountains, diving for traps is not a pleasant exercise.   In placing the bait, care must be taken to fix it just where the beaver, in reaching it, will spring the trap.   If the bait stick be placed high, the hind foot of the beaver will be caught; if low, the forefoot."

In this manner Fitzpatrick's men were now employed in the reaping of the rich harvest, though often the beaver were so plentiful that they were shot from the cover of the willows.   While the greater portion of the band was engaged in hunting, several of the men were left in camp to skin the catch, dry the hides and form them into packs, each weighing about one hundred pounds and containing about sixty pelts.

Within a week after arriving in the Green River country, the party had taken enough fur to make four packs.   Still, as they proceeded slowly down the stream, working the tributaries, the supply seemed inexhaustible — and beaver selling in St. Louis at about six dollars per pound!   One needs but little imagination to realize with what high spirits those young men pushed the work!

Another week passed.   Still the pelts accumulated amazingly, and every night brought feasting and jollity.   Within a month, at most, the band would be starting for the Pass to join Smith's party at the rendezvous on the Sweetwater.   And what a tale there would be to tell!   All the while

the busy trappers had come upon no Indian
" sign." They seemed to be the only human beings in all that vast country, though they knew
from the Crows that the tribe of Snakes claimed
the land westward from the Pass. For some
days after their arrival at the hunting grounds the
party had rigidly followed Henry's plan for making camp in a hostile territory; but soon the apparent loneliness of the region, together with the
expansive mood of success, induced laxness. Of
late, the practice of bringing the horses within the
enclosure of the camp at sunset had been discon-
tinued, and four horse-guards were deemed sufficient to watch the herd grazing out the night in
the lush bottoms near the sleeping trappers.

Now an ancient Greek would say that these
men had fallen into the great sin of hubris, being
drunk with good fortune and no longer mindful
of that humility which is befitting to the state of
mere mortals. However that may be, there came
a night when their surprising run of luck was
rudely broken, as will now appear.

They had camped in a bend of the river where
the valley broadened out, rising westward by an
easy grade to a great arid plain. The fires that
had burned merrily in the evening while the men
took their ease, smoking and yarning luxuriously,
had fallen low; and those on watch heard the snoring of the sleepers, the night wind rustling the
cottonwoods and mumbling in the willows, the con-

tented horses blowing and stamping as they nosed the fat pasture. The stars swarmed up out of the dark hollow of the world and drifted over the mysterious immensity, showering the stuff of slumber. A stricken flint spurted out yonder, and the momentary glow of a horse-guard's pipe painted a weathered face upon the gloom. A cotton-like fog crawled over the river, and the night air was tanged with a hint of frost. Hours passed, and the wheeling heavens had yet three hours to bring the dawn, when the night was suddenly filled with yelling and the sound of many galloping hoofs.

Thus rudely shaken out of deep sleep, the trappers leaped to their feet, dashing about the camp in bewilderment and shouting unanswered questions. Some of the less excitable men seized their rifles and fired into the whirlwind of shadowy horsemen that swept by, waving hide robes about their heads and howling as they circled about the panic-stricken herd and sent it stampeding up the westward slope.

It was all over before the white men fully realized what was happening. The flying shadows disappeared over the rise, and, dumfounded, the trappers stood there listening to the lessening roll of their horses' hoofs out yonder on the plain.

Here was a pretty fix, indeed! Had the horse-guards fallen asleep? That mattered little now. What mattered was the fact that the Snàkes had robbed them of their horses, and what good was all this wealth without means of transporting it over the Divide? They slept no more that night but, replenishing the fallen fires, sat down to discuss their predicament with many a lusty oath. No one had been hurt — a fact which left some room for optimism. Many of the wilder spirits were in favor of starting at once in pursuit of the animals; but Fitzpatrick saw the matter in a different light. Here was plenty of beaver; and since they had come for beaver, why not continue the hunt while the fur was good [1] and until they had all they wanted of the precious stuff? At worst, they could cache their packs, return on foot to the Sweetwater and get more horses from the Crows.

When morning came, the rich yield of the traps served to popularize Fitzpatrick's plan, and all agreed that there would be time enough to think about horses when the matter of beaver pelts had been satisfactorily handled. Further, immunity from attack by the natives of the country was fairly certain henceforth, since the Snakes had already taken what they wanted and would hardly be likely to return out of sheer wantonness.

So, not only with enthusiasm unabated, but with a heightened sense of adventure, the men went on with the trapping. The Snakes, however, remained the common topic of discussion about the

[1] Fur taken in the early spring is of finer grade than that taken in the summer.

evening fires; and more and more, as the time drew near when the need of horses should become pressing, the trappers talked of reprisal. Not only was it a long way back to the Sweetwater, but the horses that Smith had there would scarcely be sufficient for the need. As for the Crows, there was no telling where they might be with their herds during the summer — away over yonder at the Powder's mouth as like as not! Why cross the Divide? Hadn't the Snakes at least twenty five good horses? Also, weren't fourteen well-armed white men as good as a whole village of yonder rascals? Also, wouldn't it be good policy to acquaint the Snakes with the temper of the trapping breed, that future operations in the country might be attended with less annoyance?

The audacious proposal steadily gained ground among the men, until it dominated the camp. For, as a matter of fact, the rank and file of the band were far less concerned with beaver than with adventure; and here was a glorious opportunity for laying up some memories against the time when old age should make action impossible. So when twenty packs of beaver were made up, it happened that the band made ready for an expedition against the Snake tribe. This involved the making of a cache for the furs and equipment, which was done in the following manner:

Choosing a dry place in the midst of a thicket, they dug a pit six feet in diameter and eight feet deep. From this a drift was run back sufficiently large to accommodate all the impedimenta of the party. The excavation was then carefully lined with sticks and dry grass, after which the goods were carefully packed within, the opening to the drift covered with a layer of willows and grass, and the hole filled. In order that the cache might not be discovered and "lifted" by some wandering band of Indians, every particle of soil that remained was gathered up and dumped into the river, and great care was given to the replacing of the grass just as it had been before the digging. Certain bluffs, observed in relation to the spot, served as markers, and the number of days of travel from thence to the mouth of the Big Sandy would determine the general locality of the cache.

Having thus disposed of their baggage, and carrying nothing but their rifles, ammunition, and the smaller necessary articles of a trapper's equipment known as "possibles," the band started out on the trail of the Snakes which led in a northerly direction over the arid plain. There had been no rain since the night attack, and the hoofs of fifty horses (there could have been no less, counting those of the Indians) had left no doubtful record of their passing. After five long days of marching the band reached the mouth of the Sandy, and still the trail led on, skirting the Green River. It was noted that at this point the Indians had begun to travel in a leisurely manner, for the trap-

pers, though afoot, easily covered in a day the
distance from one camping ground to another; and
it became the common opinion that the Snake village could not be far away. Accordingly from
this point onward the party spent the day camping in some concealed place, and moved by night,
for the moon was full now and the trail was still
easy to follow.

Three nights they pushed on up the Green after
leaving the Big Sandy's mouth, marching from
dusk to dawn. Then, during the fourth night
when the moon in mid-heaven was flooding the
huge spaces with that purple glow that one sees
only in high dry countries and in the staging of a
melodrama, the scouts, travelling a half hour in
advance of the party, brought back a bit of news
that set all hearts pounding. Scarcely more than
a mile ahead they had looked down from a bluff
upon an Indian encampment. They had counted
twenty lodges there in an open space near the
river, and they judged that no less than one hundred horses were grazing along the bottom. On
the far side of the herd the brush seemed to be
quite dense. By passing the village and approaching the grazing horses through the brush, the
scouts judged that it would be possible for each
man to capture and mount an animal without
arousing the Indians. Then the whole herd could
be stampeded right through the village and up an
adjoining slope into the open country.

After holding a council of war, the trappers pushed on cautiously up stream, the scouts leading the way. Soon they caught the faint smell of smouldering fires, and, making a wide detour, they passed the encampment, descended into the brushy valley beyond, and crawled southward until they came to the edge of the thicket. There, within a stone's throw, was the Snake herd peacefully grazing; and, fortunately, owing to the lie of the land, the animals were well bunched. Farther on at a distance of two or three hundred yards was the dusky clutter of skin lodges, vaguely illumined here and there by glowing embers; and beyond that, where the valley turned abruptly eastward, bare bluffs sloped gradually to the plain above.

Evidently it had not occurred to the Indians that the white men might come afoot after their horses; and doubtless they knew that their ancient enemies, the Blackfeet, were hunting far away on the Missouri. The full moon clearly revealed the peaceful scene; and as the men lay there considering the situation, they gloated in whispers over the fine prospect for a clean sweep of the herd. Even the dogs had not yet sensed danger; and if any of the Indians were awake there was nothing to indicate the fact.

Now swinging their loaded rifles at their backs by means of thongs that had been prepared for this particular moment, the trappers crept on all fours out into the open and approached the herd.

Several of the nearer horses, with heads held high, ears pricked forward and tails raised, snorted alarm; and forthwith the herd crowded together and began to mill. A dog barked in the village. Now was the time! Leaping to their feet, the trappers rushed to the nearest bunch of jostling, snorting animals; and it was a tense moment during which each man, seizing the mane of a horse, scrambled to its back, knowing well what fate he might expect if he failed.

Then arose a yell that sent the herd thundering toward the encampment; and after it came the mounted trappers, howling defiance at the rudely awakened foe. Right on through the village rushed the frightened horses, making havoc among the lodges as they went; and after them rode Fitzpatrick's men, discharging their rifles as they dashed through the population of the town now swarming into the open — shrieking squaws, crying children, shouting braves, barking dogs! On up the slope beyond, the stampede thundered; and but a few minutes elapsed between the time of mounting and the moment when, topping the ridge amid a tempest of flying manes, the victors saw before them the dusky plain weird under the moon. It was an hour before the horses, fagged with the long run, fell into a jog trot and became manageable.

Morning came, and still Fitzpatrick's men pushed on southward with the herd. Nor did they venture to camp until the evening shadows began to deepen along the river valley.   Many of the horses had strayed from the herd during the wild night run, and some of those would doubtless be picked up by the Snakes before long.   Therefore haste was still necessary; and at midnight the trappers set out again into the south.   By riding the greater part of both night and day, they arrived safely at the cache during the third evening from the Indian village.

They now had forty horses in place of the twenty five so unceremoniously borrowed by the Snakes — a goodly increase on the original investment!

XIII

THE RETURN

DURING the night after they arrived at their old camp on the Green River, Fitzpatrick's men uncovered the cache and made ready for an early start next day, while the horses, carefully guarded, grazed along the bottom; and when the sun arose the band was already winding up-stream — fourteen mounted men and twenty-six pack-horses laden with the baggage and the costly bales of beaver. To follow the Green to the mouth of the Sandy would have been to risk a clash with a party of Snakes; and so, coming at noon to the mouth of a creek that entered from the east, they turned off there and followed the course of the little tributary until dusk.

They had now advanced a half day's march into an inhospitable country. Two days of travel to the northward were the headwaters of the Sandy; and when, next morning, they left the creek and ascended the low rise that bordered it, they cursed the Snakes most heartily; for they should have been following a rich valley, and now they saw ahead of them a desert country rolling drearily away to the sky-rim. Nevertheless, the prospect

offered some compensation; for though it seemed
likely that there would be no game or grass or
water yonder, neither would there be any human
foe.

All forenoon the ponies travelled northward at
a swinging walk across a baked plain of whitish
clay mixed with gravel, where even sagebrush was
scarce.   Then the soil became sandy, and soon the
party was floundering through a wilderness of
dunes where not even sagebrush grew.   With
drooping heads the sweating animals labored on
through the thirsty land.   Away to the northeast
the snow-clad mountains, tauntingly near to the
eyes but discouragingly distant for the feet, glit-
tered in the white glare of the day.   The sun
burned red over the rim of the melancholy waste,
and disappeared, and the air turned chill.   Night
without wood or water or grass!

Having paused for an hour to rest the weary
animals, the band forged ahead with their faces to
the North Star; and sullenly half the night they labored on through an empty world where the soft
padding of the hoofs and the wheezing breath of
the horses seemed very loud, so oppressive was the
stillness of that dead land.   Then when the Dipper was upside down above the Pole, the band
halted and the packs were taken off.   Until daybreak the ponies nosed and pawed the sand, nickering pitifully for grass and water.

In the white of the morning they were moving again at a slow, stumbling pace. By sunrise they had entered a rolling prairie country where once more the sagebrush grew; and when the day was half way up the sky, topping a hogback, the leading pony lifted his head and neighed; whereat the whole cavalcade, with ears pricked forward, fell to nickering joyfully, and the men shouted with them. Yonder but a mile or two away was a winding strip of green!

Soon forty horses, freed from their loads, were thrusting parched muzzles into the waters of the upper Sandy and rolling luxuriously in the green grass.

Thenceforth the trail was easy, and the party made good time up the Little Sandy, through the recently discovered pass and down the Sweetwater to the place of rendezvous. There Smith and his men were waiting, together with a band under the command of William L. Sublette, who had recently come down from the Big Horn, intending to cross the mountains if Fitzpatrick's experience in the new country should prove satisfactory.

Sublette brought the news that Major Henry had recently started down the Yellowstone for St. Louis with a boatload of furs collected at the mouth of the Big Horn during the previous fall and spring, and that he intended to return before winter with a pack-train of supplies for the men who would probably then be operating beyond the Great Divide.

Fired by the astounding stories they heard from their comrades who had just returned from the fur country of the Siskadee, Smith and Sublette decided to move westward as soon as possible, while Fitzpatrick should proceed eastward with the beaver packs.

Fitzpatrick now conceived a plan of characteristic daring. Why use horses for the trip? Many pack animals would be needed over yonder by his comrades, and to travel with a pack-train was at best a wearisome business. Why not make bullboats and drift down the Sweetwater and the Platte to the Missouri? The June flood was now on, and it seemed that such a journey should prove to be both swift and easy. The fact that no white man had yet navigated the turbulent upper portion of this long watercourse acted as a powerful argument in favor of the attempt.

Large numbers of bison were grazing in the vicinity of the rendezvous, and the three combined parties now organized a hunt; for those who were going west knew not what gameless country they might traverse in their wanderings yonder beyond the Divide; and it seemed best that here where game was abundant they should lay up a supply of dried meat against possible famine. Then, while their comrades were engaged in jerking large quantities of bison flesh, Fitzpatrick's men wrought their bullboats. John B. Wyeth,[1] who visited this region eight years later, has left us the following description of the making of a bullboat: " They first cut a number of willows about an inch and a half in diameter at the butt end, and fixed them in the ground at proper distances from each other, and as they approached each end they brought these nearer together so as to form something like the bow. The ends of the whole were bent over and bound firmly together like the ribs of a great basket; and then they took other twigs of willow and wove them into those stuck in the ground so as to make a sort of firm, huge basket twelve or fourteen feet long. After this was completed, they sewed together a number of buffalo skins, and with them covered the whole; and after the different parts had been trimmed off smooth, a slow fire was made under the bullboat, taking care to dry the skins moderately; and as they gradually dried and acquired a due degree of warmth, they rubbed buffalo tallow all over the outside of it, so as to allow it to enter into all the seams of the boat, now no longer a willow basket. As the melted tallow ran down into every seam, hole and crevice, it cooled into a firm body capable of resisting the water, and bearing a considerable blow without damaging it. Then the willow-ribbed, buffalo-skin, tallowed vehicle was carefully pulled

[1] Oregon; or a " Short History of a Long Journey from the Atlantic Ocean to the Region of the Pacific."

up from the ground, and behold a boat!" The willow ends, protruding from the rim, were then cut off and the gunwales made firm with a binding of rawhide.

Such craft, used by the Indians of the Plains before the coming of the white men, were of great service to the trappers in navigating the shoal rivers of the West; for a bullboat ten feet wide by twenty five feet long would carry over two tons with a draught of no more than four inches.

At length, when sufficient meat had been dried and two boats were launched and loaded with the Green River furs, Fitzpatrick's men, bidding farewell to their comrades who, under Smith and Sublette, were starting for the country beyond the Pass, pushed off into the swift current of the Sweetwater. All forenoon they sped along the winding stream, now in the midst of broad meadows dotted with occasional sandstone piles, carved by the wind and rain of ages into curious shapes; now plunging with the arrowy current through overhanging canyon walls fearsome with shadow and the sinister voices of the waters; now out again into the broad sunlight of a pleasant valley where bison grazed like tame cattle and bands of elk raised their heads to stare at the strange shapes that swept along the stream. Noon burned down upon the boatmen, and still they raced onward with the June rise, expressing their huge satisfaction now and then with snatches of song. Compared with the plodding pace of saddle-weary horses, this was like an indolent traveller's dream, in which hills and valleys, becoming mere pictures, obligingly moved themselves to the rear, filing past in a hushed and stately procession.

The sun was nearing the western rim and the men, congratulating themselves upon a good day's run, were thinking of camp, when they heard a low sullen roar ahead of them. Now if the day had passed in a dream of travel, yonder sound, steadily increasing in volume as they swept onward, was the voice of approaching reality, as they were very soon to realize. A few minutes later they shot out into the swirl where the Sweetwater enters the North Fork of the Platte. Then it happened!

Pressed into a rocky channel between an island and the shore, the combined floods rolled as in a great wind, though the air was still. Suddenly the leading boat reared upon a rock like a fractious horse taking a fence, caught the thrust of the current on its depressed gunwale, and capsized. In another moment the second boat had done likewise, and the turbulent channel was littered with swimming men and floating baggage.[1]

Within a few minutes all the trappers, sputtering and puffing, had reached the shore. But what

[1] In 1842 Fitzpatrick, then a member of Fremont's exploring party, was wrecked at the same place. See Fremont's "Report of the Exploring Expedition to the Rocky Mountains," Washington, 1845.

of the precious cargo and equipment?   Some of it
had gone down never to be recovered; some had
drifted into shallower water below and stranded
on the rocks.   Surely this was a rude ending for a
merry day; and right vigorously the drenched and
crestfallen trappers cursed their luck.

Having built several rousing fires on the bank
(for each had a flint and steel among his " possibles ") the men stripped, hung their buckskins up
to dry, and plunged into the swirl of cold mountain water after their baggage.   With great effort
they managed to recover the boats, some of the
equipment, and a sufficient portion of the fur to
discharge the debt to Ashley and Henry for the
outfit furnished at the mouth of the Big Horn
during the early spring.

Fitzpatrick now decided not to risk the loss of
the remaining furs by taking them down stream;
for being at that time still unfamiliar with the
North Platte, he suspected that other accidents,
such as had just occurred, might be expected before he should reach the broad, quiet waters of
the lower river.   It seemed best to hasten on with
a few men to Fort Atkinson, inform Ashley at St.
Louis as to the newly discovered hunting grounds
beyond the Divide, procure horses and return for
the furs.   So, having cached the remaining beaver
packs near the scene of the catastrophe, Fitzpatrick set out next morning with five men and one
boat, leaving the balance of the party in camp at
the mouth of the Sweetwater.

No further trouble occurred, and the light craft made good time with the high water. By travelling from daylight to dusk, in two weeks the little band reached Fort Atkinson on the Missouri. They were thus the first white men to navigate the Platte from its headwaters on the Continental Divide. At Atkinson they found a portion of the party with which General Ashley had started from St. Louis in early May. From these he learned that Major Henry, discouraged by his many misfortunes, had sold out to his partner during the previous fall and retired from the fur trade. Having ascended the Missouri with keelboats to this point, Ashley had procured horses and set out with a pack-train for the mountains by way of the Platte valley. However, shortly after reaching the Platte, a war party of Indians, probably Pawnees, had succeeded in driving off nearly all his herd, amounting to over a hundred. Thereupon Ashley, having ordered a portion of his party to return to the Missouri for more horses, while the rest remained with the baggage, had returned to St. Louis. Jim Beckwourth, who was a member of this party, tells us [1] that the General had recently been married, and returned " to transact some affairs of business and possibly to pay his devotions to his estimable lady." The " affairs of business " were concerned with Ashley's candidacy for the Governorship of Missouri, and

[1] "The Life and Adventures of James P. Beckwourth," by T. D. Bonner.

doubtless he returned for the election, which took place in August and resulted in his defeat.

Immediately upon his arrival at Fort Atkinson, Fitzpatrick wrote a letter to General Ashley at St. Louis, telling of the easy pass he had discovered, of the rich beaver country along the Green River, of his affair with the Snake Indians, and of his wreck at the mouth of the Sweetwater. Early in September, having procured a supply of horses, he set forth up the valley of the Platte to bring in his cached furs and the men he had left in camp there. The round trip was made in excellent time, for on October 26th he was back at Fort Atkinson with all his party and the pelts that had been recovered from the turbulent waters of the North Platte.

Five days before Fitzpatrick's return, General Ashley had arrived from St. Louis, intent upon starting at once for the Green River country beyond the Great Divide, that he might arrive in time for the spring hunt in which the best furs were taken. It was a daring if not a foolhardy project; for the distance to be traversed was at least eight hundred miles by the shortest possible route; winter was already beginning, and the problem of feeding both men and horses on the way was likely to prove extremely difficult.

When Ashley entered the fur trade two years before, it was his intention to operate on the upper waters of the Missouri and Yellowstone, building forts at convenient points from which his bands of trappers should receive their supplies. Also, he had hoped to penetrate the region of the upper Columbia by way of the North Pass of Lewis and Clark. But, as we have seen, his experiences on the Missouri and Yellowstone had been rather discouraging, owing to the widespread hostility of the Plains Indians, and to the formidable competition of the Missouri Fur Company. Now that Fitzpatrick had discovered a rich country beyond the Divide and an easy trail thereto, Ashley had decided to abandon the Missouri-Yellowstone region and to push operations in the new territory on a different plan. Whereas, before, he had intended to build permanent posts at various strategic points, he now decided to sweep vast scopes of country by means of wandering bands of trappers that, at a certain time each year, should bring the furs they had collected to some convenient place previously agreed upon, there to receive supplies for the following year. This annual gathering of the far-flung trappers was known as the rendezvous. Though this plan had already been employed to some extent by both the British and American traders, it was due to General Ashley's operations during the next few years that the rendezvous became one of the most important and picturesque features of the fur trade.

XIV

ASHLEY'S LONG WINTER TRAIL [1]

O N November 3rd, 1824, General Ashley left
Fort Atkinson for the far off Green River,
intending to proceed by way of the Platte, the
North Fork of the Platte, the Sweetwater, and
South Pass, which Fitzpatrick had discovered during the spring of that year.   In mid-afternoon of
the second day out he came to the mouth of the
Loup River where the greater portion of his party
had been encamped since his return to St. Louis
during the early summer.   There were twenty-
five men in this band, and they had in charge fifty
pack-horses, together with all the necessary impedimenta of a trapping expedition.   During the
summer and early fall they had fared well enough,
having succeeded in collecting a considerable quantity of beaver both by trapping and by trading
with occasional bands of Indians.   However, during the recent weeks they had been rather poorly
fed, as wild game, upon which they were forced
to depend for food, had become scarce in that re-

[1] This and the following chapter are based on General Ashley's account given in a letter to General Atkinson, dated St.
Louis, Dec. 1, 1825; *Ashley MSS*, Missouri Hist. Society. The
letter is quoted in full by Dale.

170

gion. Great was their disappointment when, after looking forward to Ashley's coming with supplies, they learned that he had brought nothing with him, but planned to purchase from the Pawnees, whose village was located some fifty miles up the Loup valley, a sufficient quantity of provisions to last until the buffalo herds should be reached. Certainly the long and hazardous journey was not beginning well. There was no singing in camp that night, and no one was in a mood for telling stories. Winter in a wild land lay ahead of these men, and there was no telling how far away the bison might be.

Of the twenty six men who sat in camp that night at the mouth of the Loup, only nine are remembered by name: General Ashley, Thomas Fitzpatrick, Robert Campbell, James P. Beckwourth, Moses Harris (generally known as " Black " Harris), one Clement (or Claymore), Baptiste La Jeunesse, one Le Brache, and one Dorway. The first three are great names in the annals of the Early West. Beckwourth, then on his first trip to the mountains, later became a chief of the Crow tribe and won great distinction among his adopted people in their many battles with the Blackfeet. At one time he was celebrated from the Missouri to the Pacific for his yarns, in all of which he figured as the hero. He is said to have been poisoned by the Crows in 1867 at a farewell dog-feast on the eve of his intended departure for his new home on Cherry Creek, Colorado; for the Crows attributed their former success in the Blackfoot wars to their white chief and wished to keep his bones among them if they could not have the living man.[1] " Black " Harris seems to have been another well known spinner of yarns, in his day, and greatly in love with the marvelous. He must have been more than ordinarily courageous and dependable, for Sublette more than once chose him for a companion on his long winter journeys. Of the last four, Clement (or Claymore) is remembered vaguely as a leader of one of the Ashley parties on Green River during the spring and summer of 1825; La Jeunesse is only a name, recorded by Beckwourth as that of his youthful friend; Le Brache did nothing more important than to get himself killed by Indians during the next summer; and Dorway, who according to Beckwourth was a Frenchman and a good swimmer, has left us nothing but his name, and even that is evidently misspelled!

Early in the morning of November 6th the party broke camp and moved up the Loup River in the direction of the Pawnee Loup village, three couriers having been sent in advance to inform the Indians that Ashley was coming to trade with them. During the afternoon it began to snow heavily from the Northeast. All night the snow

[1] " Life and Adventures of James P. Beckwourth." Coutant's " History of Wyoming " gives an account of Beckwourth's death.

fell, and all the next forenoon the string of men and horses pushed on through a white world, soundless but for the muffled footfall of the pack-animals and the whispering of the great tumbling flakes.   By noon the Northwest wind began to blow, and by dusk it was a howling fury.

During this time the rations of the men consisted of a half pint of flour per day for each man; and now that the grass was covered two feet deep, the horses were fed on cottonwood bark whenever the edible variety could be found.   However, the men struggled on in fairly good spirits, looking forward to a plenteous supply of food in the Indian town.

The 8th day of November dawned windless and bitter cold, and the men labored on patiently through the drifts up the Loup valley, thinking of the feasts they were going to have when they reached the Pawnee Loups.   It was mid-forenoon when the three couriers were seen returning along the rise that flanked the river, and these were hailed with a great cry in which the horses joined. But it was not good news that the couriers brought; for the Pawnee Loups had already left their village for their wintering ground at the Forks of the Platte.

That evening the poorest of the horses was killed for meat.

Two weeks passed by, during which frequent attempts were made to advance; but the cold was intense, the snow deep, and most of the time a blizzard wind was blowing. From the day when the first horse was killed until the 21st of November, the party was able to advance only about twelve miles. By this time many of the animals were enfeebled with hunger and cold, and several had died, their carcasses filling the kettles of the half starved men.

On the 22nd of November, the desperate party struck out across country southward and managed to reach the valley of the Platte fifteen miles away. There, by good fortune, they found an abundance of game for themselves and a good supply of rushes for the horses. Having spent all the next day in feasting about cozy fires in the protection of the timber that covered the bottom lands, they set out once more on the morning of the 24th. For ten days they toiled on up the valley of the Platte, which yielded plenty of fuel and horse feed, and their hunters kept them well supplied with the flesh of deer and elk. On December 3rd they reached Plumb Point, near the site of the present city of Kearney; and there the Grand Pawnees were encamped, being on the way to their wintering ground on the Arkansas River.

These Indians strongly advised Ashley to give up his original intention and to winter at the Forks of the Platte, which, they said, was the only place between Plumb Point and the mountains where fuel and horse feed could be found in suf-

ficient quantities. Though the weather was now
extremely cold and stormy, Ashley resumed the
march next morning. About midday the party
overtook the tribe of Pawnee Loups, whose deserted village on the Loup River had so keenly dis-
appointed the half starved trappers during the second week of November. For eight days Ashley's
men travelled in company with these Indians,
reaching the latter's wintering place at the Forks
of the Platte on December 12th. The suffering
of the men during those eight days of blizzard
weather had been intense, and half of the horses
had fallen by the way. So Ashley decided to
spend a fortnight at this place in order to purchase
horses and supplies, and to prepare his party for
the difficult journey that lay ahead, for he had
been told that little wood was to be found within
the next two hundred miles.

The weather now turned fine, and though the
hill-lands were still covered with two feet of snow,
the valleys in many places had been swept bare by
the great winds and afforded plenty of dry grass
and rushes for the horses. " The day after our
arrival at the Forks," writes Ashley, " the chiefs
and principal men of the Loups assembled in council for the purpose of learning my wants and to de-
vise means to supply them. I made known to
them that I wished to procure twenty five horses
and a few buffalo robes, and to give my men an
opportunity of providing more amply for the

further prosecution of the journey. I requested that we might be furnished with meat to subsist upon while we remained with them, and promised that a liberal remuneration should be made for any services they might render me. After their deliberations were closed, they came to this conclusion that notwithstanding they had been overtaken by unusually severe weather before reaching their wintering ground, by which they had lost a great number of horses, they would comply with my requisition in regard to horses and other necessaries as far as their means would admit. Several speeches were made by the chiefs during the council, all expressive in the highest degree of their friendly disposition toward our government, and their conduct in every particular manifested the sincerity of their declarations."

As a result of these negotiations, Ashley procured twenty three horses and a liberal supply of beans, dried pumpkin, corn, cured meat "and other necessary things." Ten days spent in resting and feasting served to put men and horses in fine spirits.

"And now," says Beckwourth,[1] "everything being ready for departure, our general intimated to Two Axe (Chief of the Loups) his wish to get on. Two Axe objected. 'My men are about to surround the buffalo,' he said; 'if you go now, you will frighten them. You must stay four days,

[1] "Life and Adventures of James P. Beckwourth," Chap. IV.

then you may go.' His word was law, so we stayed accordingly. Within the four days appointed they made the surround. There were engaged in this hunt from one to two thousand Indians, some mounted and some on foot. They encompass a large space where the buffalo are contained, and closing in around them on all points, form a complete circle. Their circle, as first enclosed, may measure perhaps six miles in diameter with an irregular circumference determined by the movements of the herd. When the surround is formed, the hunters radiate from the main body to the right and left until the ring is entire. The chief then gives the order to charge, which is communicated along the ring with the speed of lightning. Every man then rushes to the center, and the work of destruction is begun. . . . The slaughter generally lasts two or three hours. . . . The field over the surround presents the appearance of one vast slaughter house. He who has been most successful in the work of devastation is celebrated as a hero, and receives the highest honors from the fair sex, while he who has been so unfortunate as not to kill a buffalo is jeered and ridiculed by the whole band. Flaying, dressing and preserving the meat next engages their attention and affords them full employment for several weeks."

Arrangements for departure were made by Ashley's men on the 23rd of December, and on the morning of the 24th, bidding goodbye to their friends, the Pawnee Loups, they began the westward march again. It had been Ashley's intention to follow Fitzpatrick's route up the North Platte and the Sweetwater through South Pass; but the Loups had informed him that the North Fork afforded less wood than the South Fork, and accordingly he had decided to ascend the latter stream. "The weather was fine," writes 'the General, " the valleys literally covered with buffalo, and everything seemed to promise a safe and speedy movement to the first grove of timber on my route, supposed to be about ten days' march." Christmas day dawned clear, and the party continued to make good progress in the golden winter weather. During the afternoon they were overtaken by a band of Loups who had been sent out as envoys to the Arapahoes and Kiowas in the hope that they might be able to establish friendly relations between those tribes and their own people.

The next day was cloudy and bitter cold. In the afternoon it began to snow and blow again, and the night was terrible. The blizzard continued to rage until sundown of the 27th; and on the morning of the 28th four of the horses were so far gone with the cold that even when they were lifted to their feet they could not stand. Abandoning the poor brutes to the wolves, the party labored on. So deep was the snow now that had it not

been for the large herds of bison moving down the
river, progress would have been impossible.
These not only broke trail for the party, but also,
in searching for food, pawed the snow away in
many places, thus making it possible for the horses
to graze. "We continued to move forward without loss of time," writes Ashley, "hoping to be
able to reach the wood described by the Indians
before all our horses should become exhausted.
On the 1st of January, 1825, I was exceedingly
surprised and no less gratified at the sight of a
grove of timber, in appearance distant some two
or three miles on our front. It proved to be a
grove of cottonwoods of the sweetbark kind, suitable for horse food, located on an island offering,
among other conveniences, a good situation for
defence. I concluded to remain here several days
for the purpose of recruiting my horses."

At this point the five Loups bade farewell to the
white men and, each carrying on his back a small
bundle of faggots for fuel, struck southward toward the Arkansas where they expected to find the
villages of the Arapahoes and Kiowas. Ten
days were spent on the island, during which time a
strict guard was kept, as Ashley had been told that
his old enemies, the Rees, were among the Arkansas Indians. Standing guard, the general tells us,
"was much the most severe duty my men had to
perform, but they did it with alacrity and cheer-
fulness, as well as all other services required at

their hands.   Indeed, such was their pride and ambition in the discharge of their duties, that their privations in the end became sources of amusement to them."

On the 11th of January, most of the cotton-wood bark having been consumed, and the horses now being in fair condition, the party moved on up the river.   Small sticks of driftwood and some occasional willow brush served for fuel, but no edible cottonwood was found until the 20th, when they came to another island and camped.   Here, near the site of Fort Morgan, Colorado, they had their first view of the Rocky Mountains, which the General judged to be about sixty miles away.

Ashley had been informed by the Indians that it would be impossible for him to cross the mountains during the winter; so he decided to move to their base and make a fortified camp, from which trapping could be carried on while small bands were exploring the country in search of a pass through which the whole party might be taken later on.   After spending two days on the island, that the horses might recuperate, they continued their journey up the South Platte until they reached a stream coming in from a northwesterly direction.[1]   Ascending this tributary (doubtless the Cache La Poudre), they camped on the 4th of February " in a thick grove of cottonwood and

[1] Up to this point Ashley had been following Major Long's route of the summer of 1820; henceforth his journey was through an unknown country.

willows " among the foothills of the Front Range. Long's Peak loomed huge to southward, seeming to Ashley no more than six or eight miles away, though the distance must have been at least thirty-five miles.

After leaving the camp of January 20th, game had become scarcer and scarcer, and the party had been forced to rely almost entirely upon the provisions that had been procured from the Loups at the Forks of the Platte.

The main body remained in camp here for three weeks, during which time small detachments were busily engaged in exploring. Finally, on the 26th of February, Ashley began the passage of the foothills, though the country was still " enveloped in one mass of snow and ice." " Our passage across the first range of mountains, which was exceedingly difficult and dangerous," so runs the General's narrative, " employed us three days, after which the country presented a different aspect. Instead of finding the mountains more rugged as I advanced towards their summit and everything in their bosom frozen and torpid, affording nothing on which an animal could possibly subsist, they assumed quite a different character. The ascent of the hills (for they do not deserve the name of mountains) was so gradual as to cause but little fatigue in travelling over them. The valleys and south sides of the hills were but partially covered with snow, and the latter presented already in a slight degree the verdure of spring, while the former were filled with numerous herds of buffalo, deer and antelope."

The party had now crossed from the country drained by the South Platte to that drained by the North Platte. Travelling slowly northwest by west for nine days through a region almost destitute of wood, they came on the 10th of March to a stream " about one hundred feet wide, meandering north-eastwardly through a beautiful and fertile valley about ten miles in width." This was the Laramie River, and here two days were spent in camp, as the valley furnished a fairly good supply of dry grass for the horses and an abundance of fuel.

Moving again on the 12th of March, the party camped in the evening at the foot of the Medicine Bow Mountains, which Ashley attempted to cross on the 14th and 15th; but finding the snow from three to five feet deep, he gave up the attempt and returned to his former camping place. Having rested a day, the party set out on the 17th, travelling northwardly along the base of the range. " As I thus advanced," writes the General, " I was delighted with the variegated scenery presented by the valleys and mountains, which were enlivened by innumerable herds of buffalo, antelope and mountain sheep grazing on them; and what added no small degree of interest to the whole scene were the many small streams issuing from the mountains, bordered with a thin growth of small willows and richly stocked with beaver. As my men could profitably employ themselves on these streams, I moved slowly along, averaging no more than five or six miles per day, and sometimes remained two days at the same encampment."

On the 21st of March, the appearance of the country seemed to justify another attempt to cross the mountains; and on the afternoon of the 23rd, after struggling through a " rough and broken country generally covered with snow," the party camped " on the edge of a beautiful plain," with the Medicine Bow range behind them.

Moving westward across the plain on the 24th, they camped for the night on the North Platte, a few miles south of the point where the Union Pacific Railroad now crosses that stream. The 25th and 26th days of March were spent in passing over an " elevated rough country entirely destitute of wood and affording no water save what could be procured by the melting of snow." Sage brush was used for fuel.

During the next five days the party pushed across the Great Divide Basin, " which appeared to have no outlet," and succeeded in crossing the Continental Divide at a point that later came to be known as Bridger's Pass.

During the night of the 2nd of April a party of Crow Indians, returning from an expedition against the Snakes, drove off seventeen of the white men's horses and mules, leaving the party in a "dreadful condition," as the General tells us. With one man, Ashley boldly pursued the thieves and recovered three of the animals that had strayed from the stolen herd. On the 4th of April, nine men were sent out in pursuit of the Crows, while Ashley, with the balance of the party, laden with the packs of the stolen horses, "proceeded in search of a suitable encampment at which to await the return of the horse-hunters." On the 6th Ashley's weary band reached a small stream running northwest, which is now called Morton Creek. Here they found the first running water and the first wood since leaving their camp of March 24th on the North Platte. About ten miles farther on down stream they reached another creek, later known as the Big Sandy, down which Fitzpatrick had led his men just one year before. Here they remained in camp until the 11th of April, when the nine men, who had been sent in pursuit of the Crows, returned without horses. On the 12th the party started down the Sandy, making no more than eight miles a day, for the men were heavily laden and the weather was snowy and raw. After travelling down the stream for six days, they struck across country to the westward, and in the evening of April 18th, 1825, they went into camp on the banks of "a beautiful river running south." They had reached the Green one hundred sixty-six days after leaving Fort Atkinson on the Missouri!

Thus ended one of the most remarkable journeys in the annals of the West. Commenting thereon, Harrison Clifford Dale says: " In 1824–25, Ashley plotted the first section of the central overland route to the Pacific. . . . He was the first white man to travel this route in the dead of winter, and the first to use that variation of South Pass, called by the name of one of his employees, James Bridger. He was the first American to investigate the mountains of northern Colorado, the first to enter the Great Divide Basin, to cross almost the entire length of southern Wyoming, and the first to navigate the dangerous canyons of Green River." [1]

The latter exploit will be considered in the following chapter.

[1] "The Ashley-Smith Explorations," page 116.

XV

DOWN GREEN RIVER

AFTER a whole winter of difficult travel through a wild country, much of which no white man had ever seen before, Ashley had reached the chosen trapping ground with his party afoot and heavily burdened. Obviously, men who were playing the rôle of the pack-horse could not be expected to explore a wide scope of country in search of furs, and it became necessary to cache the merchandise at some convenient place, that the horses, which the Crows had failed to drive off, might be used by the trappers. However, the point at which Ashley was then camped was too far north for his purposes; for he wished to explore the country to the southward which no white man had yet penetrated. The General therefore decided to build a bullboat, descend the Green to " some eligible point about one hundred miles below," there to deposit the greater portion of the merchandise, " and make such marks as would designate it as a place of general rendezvous."

Three days were spent in camp, during which some of the men were engaged in making a frame for the boat, while others were sent out to procure bison hides for the covering. When the boat was completed and loaded with the packs, Ashley divided his party into four bands. One of six men was to proceed to the sources of the Green; another of seven was to explore the region of the Bear River range to the westward; and a third group of six was to push southward toward the Uinta Mountains. The leaders of the bands, only two of whom are known — Fitzpatrick and one Clement (or Claymore)—" were instructed to endeavor to fall in with " the parties of Jedediah Smith and William Sublette who, as we have noted, had set out for the country beyond South Pass at the time when Fitzpatrick began his disastrous voyage down the Sweetwater. All the Ashley men then in the mountains were to assemble by the 10th of July at a point to be marked by the General farther down the Green.

All preparations having been made, the three bands, with the horses, left camp on Thursday, April 21st, 1825; and Ashley, with the six remaining men, began his voyage.

" After making about fifteen miles," so runs the narrative, "we passed the mouth of the creek which we had left on the morning of the 18th, and to which we gave the name of Sandy." Thus was named a stream destined to become famous in the great days of the California and Oregon Trail, when migrating thousands should pour down upon it through South Pass.

Soon after pushing off that morning, it had become evident to Ashley's little band that the boat was too heavily laden for safety, if, as might be expected, there should be rapids ahead.   So, having decided to build another boat, they went into camp at four o'clock in the afternoon some twenty five miles below the Sandy.   The new craft was finished by the evening of the 23rd, and on Sunday morning, the 24th, they were off again, making thirty miles before they tied up for the night.

During the 25th, they drifted rapidly through twenty miles of " mountainous country," passed the mouth of " a beautiful, bold-running stream about fifty yards wide " (now called Black's Fork), and camped on an island " after making about twenty five miles." For five days thereafter they moved on down stream in a leisurely fashion " without observing any remarkable difference in the appearance of the river or the surrounding country."   On the last day of April they " arrived at the base of a lofty mountain, the summit of which was covered with snow," and camped at the mouth of " a creek sixty feet wide " (now known as Henry's Fork), that entered from the west.   " This spot," says Ashley, " I selected as a place of general rendezvous, which I designated by marks in accordance with the instruction given to my men."

Thus far no difficulty had been encountered in the descent of the river, for the channel, in the most shallow places, had been no less than four feet deep. Game had been abundant, for bison were at that time " travelling from the west in great numbers."

Having spent the 1st of May at the mouth of Henry's Fork, they pushed off again on the 2nd, and had proceeded only about a half mile when the mountains closed in on either side of the river, rising perpendicularly to a height of one thousand five hundred feet. The channel narrowed to half its former width; the current became swifter; and the moaning sound of shadowy waters filled the winding gorge into which the boatmen now rushed, ignorant of what might lie ahead and unable to stop had they wished to do so. At length, rounding a bend, the boats swept out into a place where the huge walls fell back, leaving a pleasant little park along the margins of the stream. But scarcely had the boatmen felt relief from dread, when, swerving sharply to the left, the moaning current swirled them into a second fearsome gorge cut sheer through a lofty mountain. Once again they emerged into an open space, and once again the dark waters swept them onward through an overhanging canyon. And when they emerged again into an open space some ten miles below the mouth of Henry's Fork, they decided to call it a day, and camped. They had that day passed through the three canyons now called Flaming Gorge, Horseshoe, and Kingfisher.

Putting off in the morning of the 3rd of May, which was Sunday, they found the river " remarkably crooked with more or less rapids every mile, caused by rocks which had fallen from the sides of the mountain," and these made brisk work for the crews.   They had made about twenty miles from their last camp when, hearing a deep roar of waters in the defile ahead of them, they hastily rowed to shore.   Cautiously working their way along the bank, they " descended to the place from whence the danger was to be apprehended.   It proved to be a perpendicular fall of ten or twelve feet produced by large fragments of rocks which had fallen from the mountain and settled in the river, extending entirely across the channel and forming an impregnable barrier to the passage of loaded watercraft."   So they were obliged to unload their boats and let them down over the falls by means of long lines which they had provided for that purpose.   It was sunset when this operation had been completed and the boats reloaded. Dropping down stream about a mile, they camped for the night.   The falls over which they had passed have been given the name of their discoverer.

During his stop at this point, Ashley painted his name and the year on a huge bowlder that had fallen from the canyon wall, and the first three letters were still visible when the Kolb Brothers

passed that way in 1911.[1]   The inscription was
seen by William L. Manly in 1840,[2] and by J. W.
Powell in 1869.[3]

   During the 4th of May the boats sped safely
onward in the midst of lofty heights " almost entirely composed of strata of rock of various colors
(mostly red) and partially covered with a dwarf-
ish growth of pine and cedar."   In the morning
of the 5th, having dropped six miles down stream,
they came to a place where " the mountains gradually recede from the water's edge, and the river
expands to the width of two hundred fifty yards,
leaving the bottoms on each side from one to three
hundred yards wide, interspersed with clusters of
small willows."   This little valley, surrounded by
lofty mountain walls, later came to be known as
Brown's Hole.   There Ashley's party remained
in camp until the morning of the 7th of May,

   [1] "Through the Grand Canyon from Wyoming to Mexico,"
by E. L. Kolb. New York, 1914.
   [2] "Death Valley in 1849," by William L. Manly, San José,
1894.
   [3] "Exploration of the Colorado of the West," by J. W. Powell.
Washington, 1878.

when, descending ten miles, they camped " on a spot of ground where several thousand Indians had wintered. Many of their lodges remained as perfect as when occupied. They were made of poles two or three inches in diameter, set up in circular form, and covered with cedar bark."

The adventurers had proceeded but two miles on the 8th when once again they were swept into a narrow winding canyon (now called Lodore), the sides of which rose gloomily to a tremendous height. Says Ashley: " As we passed along between these massy walls, which in a great degree excluded from us the rays of heaven and presented a surface as impassable as their body was impregnable, I was forcibly struck with the gloom which spread over the countenances of my men. They seemed to anticipate (and not far distant too) a dreadful termination of our voyage, and I must confess that I partook in some degree of what I supposed to be their feelings, for things around us had truly an awful appearance. We soon came to a dangerous rapid which we passed over with a slight injury to our boats. A mile lower down, the channel became so obstructed by the intervention of large rocks over and between which the water dashed with such violence as to render our passage in safety impracticable. The cargoes of our boats were therefore a second time taken out and carried about two hundred yards, to which place, after much labor, our boats were descended by means of cords." About fifteen miles farther down stream they passed the mouth of the Yampa, which Ashley named Mary's River.

Within the next few days the party succeeded in reaching the mouth of the Uinta River (which, according to Ashley, the Indians called the Tewinty), having run the rapids of Whirlpool Canyon, " where the mountains again close to the water's edge and are more terrific than any seen during the whole voyage." There, near the site of the present town of Ouray, Utah, Ashley's men cached the cargoes of their boats, as the General had decided to ascend the Uinta River to its source on the return trip to the place of rendezvous. They then continued the descent of the Green River, passing through Desolation Canyon to a point about fifty miles below the mouth of the Uinta, the river being bounded all the way " by lofty mountains heaped together in the greatest disorder, exhibiting a surface as barren as can be imagined."

They had been travelling for three weeks down the Green River (never before navigated by white men), and now coming to the conclusion that nothing was to be gained by continuing the voyage, they abandoned their boats and started back afoot for their cache at the mouth of the Uinta. Within a few days they fell in with a friendly band of Utah Indians. " I understood by signs from them," says Ashley, " that the river which I had descended, and which I supposed to be the Rio

Colorado of the West,[1] continued its course as far
as they had any knowledge of it, southwest
through a mountainous country.   They also informed me that all the country known to them
south and west from the Tewinty River was almost entirely destitute of game, that the Indians
inhabiting that region subsist principally on roots,
fish and horses."

Having procured horses from the Utahs, the
white men pushed on to the mouth of the Uinta,
loaded their animals with the merchandise that
had been cached there, and proceeded up the
Uinta to the mouth of the Duchesne, which they
followed through a mountainous and sterile country to its headwaters.   From thence they
crossed the Uinta Mountains and came upon the
upper tributaries of the Weber River, which Ashley took to be the Buenaventura, a mythical stream
then supposed to flow into the Bay of San Francisco!   After travelling sixty miles down the
Weber, they fell in with a portion of the band that
had set out with Smith and Sublette from the camp
on the Sweetwater during the previous summer.
With this band were twenty nine men who had deserted from the Hudson Bay Company and were
now bringing their furs to the rendezvous of the
American trappers.   From these and from a band
of Utahs recently encountered, Ashley gained the

[1] Above the mouth of the Grand River the Rio Colorado of
the West is called Green River.

impression that the stream he had been following emptied into a lake, from the western end of which a great river flowed westward to the sea. " The necessity of my unremitted attention to my business," writes Ashley, " prevented me from gratifying a great desire to descend the river to the ocean, which I ultimately declined with the greatest reluctance." It will be noted from this remark how little was then known of the vast central country between the Continental Divide and the Pacific. Ashley could not guess that he was then seven hundred miles distant from the ocean by an air-line route, and that in all the vast triangular space between the Snake and the Colorado no river rising in the Rockies reached the sea.

From the camp on the Weber, the combined parties set out for the appointed place of rendezvous.

XVI

THE RENDEZVOUS

TEN weeks had elapsed since Ashley's party had separated into four bands and struck out in as many directions from the camp on the Green River fifteen miles above the Sandy's mouth; and now all the trappers employed by Ashley in that country, including the parties of Smith and Sublette who had wintered west of the Divide, began to arrive at the place of rendezvous, their pack-animals laden with the precious spoils of many a beaver stream. By the 1st of July, 1825, one hundred twenty men, including the twenty-nine who had deserted from the Hudson Bay Company, were encamped on the Green at the mouth of Henry's Fork. Beckwourth tells us that many of the Frenchmen had their squaws and children with them, and that the encampment was " quite a little town."

When all had come in, the General opened his goods, " consisting of flour, sugar, coffee, blankets, tobacco, whisky, and all other articles necessary for that region." Whereupon, so Beckwourth assures us, the jubilee began. Some of these men had left St. Louis with Henry in the spring of 1822 and had been in the wilderness ever since. Many had not tasted sugar or coffee for many months, having lived entirely on the game of the country, and tobacco and whisky were luxuries not to be despised. These articles were purchased at enormous prices, and many a trapper not only swallowed in a day of ease what he had earned in a year of constant danger and hardship, but when the rendezvous broke up found himself indebted to his employer for his next year's outfit. Story-telling, gambling, drinking, feasting, horse-racing, wrestling, boxing, and target-shooting were the order of the day —" all of which were indulged in with a heartiness that would astonish more civilized societies," says Beckwourth.

The free trappers, who were not paid by the year as were the hired trappers, but, being their own masters, trapped where they pleased and sold their furs at the annual rendezvous, were the " cocks of the walk." These boasted freely with the naïveté of children — or Homeric heroes. As Joseph Meek tells us: " They prided themselves on their hardihood and courage; even on their recklessness and profligacy. Each claimed to own the best horses; to have had the wildest adventures; to have made the most narrow escapes; to have killed the greatest number of bears and Indians; to be the greatest favorite with the Indian belles, the greatest consumer of alcohol, and to have the most money to spend — that is,

the largest credit on the books of the company.
If his hearers did not believe him, he was ready to
run a race with them, to beat them at 'cold
sledge,' or to fight, if fighting were preferred —
ready to prove what he affirmed in any way the
company pleased." [1]

While this orgy proceeds and the year's business is being transacted, let us see what of permanent value these men had accomplished in their
wanderings; for it is not because they brought
back much beaver that we remember them now.

A year has passed since we last saw Jedediah
Smith and William L. Sublette. They were then
pushing westward up the Sweetwater with a string
of pack-horses and about fifty men, and they had
just said farewell to Fitzpatrick bound by boat for
Fort Atkinson with the proceeds of his spring
hunt. Having crossed South Pass and followed
the Little and Big Sandys down to the Green, the
party was divided into three bands — one under
Sublette, one under Etienne Provost, and one, consisting of only six men, under Jedediah Smith.
From this point Smith turned northward, moving
slowly and trapping as he went, following the
course of the Green River to the mouth of Horse
Creek, which comes in from the west at a point
slightly south of the 43rd parallel. Ascending
this stream to its source, he crossed over to the
headwaters of Hoback's River which he descended

[1] Victor. "The River of the West." Chap. I.

to the Snake River. After travelling about one hundred miles down the latter stream, he turned northward, striking across country in the direction of Clark's Fork of the Columbia. He was now well into the territory that was being worked by the roving bands of the Hudson Bay Company, operating from various posts, the chief of which was Fort Vancouver on the lower Columbia. Previous to leaving the Snake River, he had been travelling practically the same route that had been followed by the eastbound Astorians under Robert Stuart just twelve years before. Buffalo were plentiful all along the way, so that the little party suffered no want. Also, many streams rich in beaver had been found, and by the end of summer Smith's horses were fairly well loaded with pelts.

Then one day in early fall a band of Iroquois Indians, led by a Canadian half-breed named Pierre, came to Smith's camp in a most wretched condition. They were without horses and guns, and were on the verge of starvation. Smith learned from them that they had started during February of that year from Spokane House on the Spokane River, a branch of the upper Columbia, with a party of Hudson Bay Company men under Alexander Ross, bound for the buffalo country at the headwaters of the Missouri and Yellowstone. They had crossed the Bitter Root Mountains and the Continental Divide with Ross during the winter, had hunted in the region of the

Three Forks of the Missouri during the spring, and then, swinging southward and westward through what is now called the Yellowstone National Park, had begun to trap on the upper waters of the Snake. During June they had been detached from the main party and sent southward. All summer long they had wandered about, taking many beaver; but a week or two before falling in with the Americans, they had been attacked by a band of Snake Indians and had been robbed of horses, guns, and most of their peltry. However, they still had nine hundred skins, worth at that time in St. Louis not less than $5,000.

Now Smith was both a Christian and a Yankee. Being a Christian, he could do no less than give succor to those in distress; being a Yankee, he drove a hard bargain at the same time. He would escort the Iroquois to Pierre's Hole where Alexander Ross was thought to be encamped with the main party, and for such services he would accept the nine hundred skins in advance! At least, such was the story the Indians told to Ross. The unfortunate Indians, having accepted Smith's proposition, all the furs thus far acquired were cached, and the two parties started for Pierre's Hole. They had travelled only a few days when they met a band of Hudson Bay men who had been sent out to find the missing Iroquois, and by these Smith was guided to Ross's camp on the Salmon River near the mouth of the Pashimari.

It was now the middle of October, 1824 — about the time when Ashley at Fort Atkinson on the Missouri was preparing for his long winter journey up the Platte and across the Rockies to the Green River. Alexander Ross was ready to start for Flathead House, a Hudson Bay Company post on the upper waters of Clark's Fork of the Columbia, and Smith decided to accompany him, being eager to view the country and wishing to learn as much as possible about the doings of the British traders in that region. Surely our hero did not lack audacity!

On November 1st Ross's party, with their self-invited American guests, crossed the Bitter Root Mountains, by the same route that Lewis and Clark had taken nineteen years before, and reached Flathead House on November 26th. On the same day Peter Skeene Ogden, one of the greater leaders of the Hudson Bay Company, arrived from Spokane House with an expedition bound for the Snake River country. Ogden remained there until December 20th, when he started for the spring trapping grounds. It is believed that Smith, having gathered all the information possible during his month's sojourn at Flathead House, accompanied Ross southward up the Bitter Root River to its source, thence across the divide to the Salmon River.

Early in the spring of 1825 Smith and his men, after recovering the peltry they had cached dur-

ing the previous fall, arrived in Cache Valley
slightly below the point where the Bear River,
flowing southward, crosses the Utah line. Here
they met Sublette's party, and it is easy to imagine
with what eagerness the reunited comrades told
of their adventures and wanderings.

Sublette and his men had been on a wild goose
chase, though they too had succeeded in taking
much fur by the way. Striking south and west
from the mouth of the Sandy, where they had said
farewell to the parties under Provost and Smith
during the summer of 1824, they had come upon
the upper waters of the Bear River which they
took to be the Buenventura. They had followed
this river throughout the remainder of the summer, trapping as they went. Rounding the
Wasatch Mountains on the north and following
the stream westward and southward, they had
reached Cache Valley late in the fall, and finding
it a sheltered place with plenty of wood, they had
decided to winter there.

During the winter there had been much discussion among Sublette's men as to what would
be found at the mouth of the stream upon which
they were encamped, and by way of settling the
discussion James Bridger, then but twenty years
old, had descended Bear River to its mouth, where,
quite naturally, he had found salt water! Returning to winter quarters, he reported to his companions what he had discovered, and it was be-

lieved that he had actually reached an arm of the
Pacific Ocean!

The party under Provost, after parting from
their comrades at the Sandy's mouth, had pushed
southward for a considerable distance along the
Green during the late summer of 1824; then turning westward, they had crossed the upper waters
of the Bear and reached the Weber, which also
empties into Salt Lake, but by a much more direct
route than that of the Bear. Believing that he
was on the Buenaventura, Provost descended the
Weber; but how far he proceeded before going
into winter quarters is unknown.   There seems to
be some reason to suspect that he may have
reached Great Salt Lake in the fall of 1824, and
that he spent the winter there near the Weber's
mouth, thus antedating Bridger's discovery by a
few months; but proof is wanting. At least it is
known that Provost's band was at the mouth of
the Weber early in the spring. Also, Jedediah
Smith, so Ashley tells us in his letter to General
Atkinson, had fallen " on the waters of the Grand
Lake of Buenaventura " (meaning Great Salt
Lake) on his return from Flathead House before
he reached Cache Valley.

Thus, within a few months, three of the Ashley
bands had reached Great Salt Lake by different
routes. However, James Bridger is generally
considered the discoverer.

During the spring hunt of 1825 a band of

Hudson Bay men, that had been sent southward by Ogden from the upper Snake River country where he was then operating, fell in with a small detachment of Ashley men under Johnson Gardner on the Bear River. Gardner induced the British trappers to desert their employer and bring their catch (worth a fortune) to the American rendezvous. These were the men whom Ashley met, in company with one of his own bands, on the upper reaches of the Weber during June. Happily, Gardner's right to be remembered does not rest wholly upon this rather questionable transaction. His name goes linked with that of Hugh Glass; for in the winter of 1832 when Glass was killed by his old enemies, the Rees, on the frozen Yellowstone, not far below the mouth of the Big Horn, it was Johnson Gardner who, according to the famous traveller, Maximilian, Prince of Wied-Neuwied, followed the murderers and " killed two of them with his own hands." [1]

And now all the Ashley men, who had been widely scattered in seven bands, were reunited on the Green River at the mouth of Henry's Fork, having explored the country bordering the Rockies on the west from the upper waters of Clark's Fork of the Columbia in latitude 47° 30′, to a point slightly below latitude 40° on the Green River.

[1] " Maximilian's Travels in North America," page 304. Beckwourth also tells the story in Chapter XVII of the " Life and Adventures."

Let us note the significance of what these men were doing.

In 1792 Captain Gray of the Boston trading ship, *Columbia,* had discovered the mouth of the great river which he named after his vessel. In 1805 Lewis and Clark had crossed the Continental Divide from the headwaters of the Missouri River and had descended the Columbia to the Pacific. In the fall of 1810 Major Andrew Henry, as we have noted, had crossed the Continental Divide and built a trading post on Henry's Fork of the Snake River, but owing to the hostility of the Blackfeet he had been forced to abandon his position the next year. In 1811 John Jacob Astor's men had founded the fur-trading establishment of Astoria at the Columbia's mouth. Thus by right of discovery, exploration, and occupation, the Americans claimed the great Oregon country lying west of the Rockies and north of latitude 42°, the northern boundary of the Spanish domain. But *possession* was quite another matter. In 1814, as a result of the war with England, Astor's great enterprise had failed, and the British Northwest Company had taken possession of Astoria, renaming it Fort George. Since that time English traders — first the Northwest Company, then the Hudson Bay Company — had been " the lords of the land," although an agreement had been made in 1818 whereby the British and the Americans were to have equal rights in the Oregon country. But so long as the Americans knew no overland route save those that had been followed by Lewis and Clark and by the Astorians, "joint occupancy" virtually meant British occupancy; for the northern passes across the Rockies were very difficult to cross, and the inveterate hostility of the Blackfeet made that way extremely hazardous. Had not a more advantageous road been found across the Continental Divide during those early years, it is most probable that the English would have become permanently established throughout the territory drained by the Columbia system; for always the flag follows the trader.

Thomas J. Farnham, who travelled overland to Oregon in 1839–40, when the stream of emigration was already beginning to flow across the Rockies, made the following just observations regarding the great central route to the Pacific: " The Platte, therefore, when considered in relation to our intercourse with the habitable countries of the Western Ocean, assumes an unequalled importance among the streams of the Great Prairie wilderness. But for it, it would be impossible for man or beast to travel those arid plains, destitute, alike, of wood, water, and grass, save what of each is found along its course. Upon the headwaters of the North Fork too is the only way or opening in the Rocky Mountains at all practicable for a carriage road through them.

That travelled by Lewis and Clark is covered with perpetual snow; that near the debouchure of the South Fork of the river is over high and nearly impassable precipices; that travelled by myself, farther south, is, and ever will be impassable for wheel carriages. But the Great Gap (South Pass) seems designed by nature as the great gateway between the nations on the Atlantic and Pacific Oceans."[1]

Dr. John McLoughlin, factor of the Hudson Bay Company's post, Fort Vancouver, used to say: " For all coming time we and our children will have uninterrupted possession of this country, as it can never be reached by families but by water around Cape Horn." And upon being told that he would live to see the coming of the Yankees, he would answer: " As well might they undertake to go to the moon! "[2] He was thinking of the northern passes.

But now Ashley's men under Fitzpatrick had found a great natural road leading up the valleys of the Platte and the Sweetwater, over the scarcely noticeable Divide at South Pass; and Ashley himself had travelled a variation of this route by way of the South Platte and Bridger's Pass. The gateway of the mountains had swung open at last, and henceforth there would be no lack of Americans in the country west of the Rockies. It was

[1] " Travels in the Great Western Prairies."
[2] Clarke. " Pioneer Days of Oregon History."

the beginning of the invasion of the Far West. In course of a few years the settlers would follow the trail of the trappers in ever increasing numbers, until, when the river of humanity should be in full flood forty years later, ten thousand wagons, bound for Oregon and California, would trundle up that way in a single season.[1]

Down from the North as far as Snake River had come the English. Up from the South, penetrating the wilderness as far as Utah Lake, and spreading up the coast of California, had come the Spaniards. Between the countries known to the British and the Spanish lay an unknown land. And now, at the Green River rendezvous in July, 1825, already were gathered together some of those who, within the next two years, were destined to lift the veil of mystery from that vast triangular space.

[1] Oberholzer. " A History of the United States Since the Civil War." Macmillan, 1917. Vol. I, page 304.

XVII

BACK TO THE STATES

ASHLEY'S luck which, as we have seen, had been bad enough so long as he operated east of the Rockies, had now turned. Not only had his own bands brought in a large quantity of beaver to the Green River rendezvous, but from the twenty nine Hudson Bay Company trappers, who had deserted from Ogden's party, he had procured a fortune " for a mere song," as he is said to have remarked. Says Beckwourth: " There lay the General's fortune in one immense pile, collected at the expense of severe toil, privation, suffering, peril, and, in some cases, loss of life. The skins he had purchased from Ogden's men and from free trappers had cost him comparatively little. If he should meet with no misfortune on his way to St. Louis, he would receive enough to pay all his debts and have an ample fortune besides." The exact quantity of beaver fur collected by Ashley at the rendezvous of 1825 is not known. Contemporary estimates vary from forty to one hundred thirty packs of one hundred pounds each, the valuation ranging from $40,000 to $200,000. It is probable that he collected no less than $100,000 worth of furs — an imposing fortune in those days when the purchasing power of a dollar was far greater than now.

" The packs were all arranged," continues Beckwourth, " and our Salt Lake friends (the deserters) offered him (Ashley) the loan of all the horses he wanted, and engaged to escort him to the Wind River." All preparations for the return to St. Louis being completed, Ashley bade farewell to those who were remaining in the country, and set out with a large pack-train and fifty men, half of the latter being Ogden's trappers who would return with the horses after the General had reached a point on the Big Horn from whence he could proceed by water to the States. Jedediah Smith was one of those who were chosen to accompany the General to St. Louis.

It is probable that Ashley would have attempted to navigate the Sweetwater and the Platte, had not Fitzpatrick's voyage of the previous summer resulted in disaster. He himself was unfamiliar with the Big Horn and the Yellowstone, having ascended with Major Henry only to the mouth of the latter river in 1822; but a number of those who were now returning with him had ascended the Yellowstone with Henry in the fall of 1823, and had followed up the Big Horn on their way to South Pass during the spring and summer of 1824.

Following the Green northward from Henry's Fork to the mouth of the Big Sandy, Ashley's party ascended the latter and, crossing the Great Divide at South Pass, came on the upper reaches of the Sweetwater. Here the main body with the pack animals turned northward toward the Popo Agie, while Ashley, with twenty men and twice as many horses, proceeded down stream in order to recover forty-five packs of beaver that Sublette's party had collected, during the spring hunt of 1824, and cached before pushing on across the mountains to the Green during the following summer.

Within a few days after separating from the main party, Ashley's men had raised the cache and started in a northwesterly direction to rejoin their comrades on the Wind River, when they were attacked by a band of Blackfeet three times their own in number. " They made their appearance at the break of day, yelling in the most hideous manner," writes Ashley [1], " and using every means in their power to alarm our horses, which they so effectually did that the horses, although closely hobbled, broke by the guard and ran off. A part of the Indians being mounted, they succeeded in getting all the horses but two, and wounded one man. An attempt was also made to take our camp, but in that they failed."

During the next night Ashley sent out a small

[1] Letter to General Atkinson, previously quoted.

band to find the main body of trappers and bring
back horses with which to transport the furs.
Knowing the character of Jed Smith, it seems a
reasonable guess that he led this band.   During
the second day after the battle the little party
returned safely with the necessary animals, and
Ashley proceeded on his way, none the worse for
his encounter with the Blackfeet.   After making
about ten miles, he camped.   " That night about
twelve o'clock," the General tells us, " we were
again attacked by a party of Crow Indians."
Again Beckwourth, who was with Ashley, is on
hand with the particulars: " I and my boy Baptiste (La Jeunesse) were sleeping among the
packs, as were also some of the other men, when
the sentinel came to me to tell me that he had
seen something which he believed to be Indians.
I arose and satisfied myself that he was correct.
I sent a man to acquaint the General, at the same
time awaking the boy and two men near me.   We
noiselessly raised ourselves, took as good aim as
possible, and, at a signal from me, all four fired.
We saw two men run.   By this time the whole
camp was aroused. . . . Our whole force was on
guard from that time till the morning, when we
discovered two dead Indians lying where we had
directed our aim in the night.   We at first supposed the two Indians belonged to the Blackfeet,
but we subsequently found they were Crows.
One of them wore a fine pair of buckskin leggings,

which I took from him and put on myself."

During the day after this slight affair, Ashley's band overtook the main party, probably near the mouth of the Popo Agie, which flows northwardly into the Wind River. Shortly after this, while the reunited bands were moving down the Wind River, they encountered a large band of Indians. Again Beckwourth will oblige us: " The alarm was given, and, on looking out, we saw an immense body of them, well mounted, charging directly down upon our camp. Every man seized his rifle and prepared for the living tornado. The General gave orders for no man to fire until he did. By this time the Indians were within half pistol-shot. Greenwood (one of our party) pronounced them Crows and called out several times not to shoot. We kept our eyes upon our General; he pulled trigger, but his gun missed fire, and our camp was immediately filled with their warriors. Most fortunate it was for us that the General's gun did miss fire, for they numbered over a thousand, and not a man of us would have escaped to see the Yellowstone.

" Greenwood, who knew the Crows, acted as interpreter between our General and the Indian chief, whose name was Absaroka Betetsa, Sparrow-Hawk Chief. After making numerous inquiries about our success in hunting, the chief inquired where we were from.

" ' From Green River,' was the reply.

" ' You killed two Blackfeet? '

" ' Yes.'

" ' Where are their scalps?   My people want to dance.'

" ' Don't show them! ' cried Greenwood to us.

" Turning to the Indian: ' We did not take their scalps.'

" ' Ugh!   That is strange.'

" During this colloquy I had buried my scalp in the sand, and concealed my leggings, knowing they had belonged to a Crow.   The chief gave orders to his warriors to move on, many of them keeping with us on our road to their camp, which was but a short distance off.   Soon after reaching there, an Indian woman issued from a lodge and approached the chief.   She was covered with blood, and, crying in the most piteous tones, she addressed the chief: ' These are the men who killed my son, and will you not avenge his death? ' She was almost naked, and, according to their custom when a near relative is slain, had inflicted wounds all over her body in token of her deep mourning.   The chief turned to the General, then said: ' The two men who were killed in your camp were not Blackfeet but my own warriors; they were good horse thieves and brave men. One of them was a son of this woman, and she is crying for his loss.   Give her something to make her cease her cries, for it angers me to see her grief.'

" The General cheerfully made her a present of what things he had at hand, to the value of about $50. ' Now,' said the chief to the woman, ' go to your lodge and cease your crying.' She went away seemingly satisfied.

" During the day two other Indians came to the encampment, and, displaying each a wound, said : ' See here what you white people have done to us. You shot us; white people shoot good in the dark.' The General distributed some presents among these two men. Happening to look among their numerous horses, we recognized some that had been stolen from us previous to our reaching Green River.[1] The General said to the chief : ' I believe I see some of my horses among yours.'

" ' Yes, we stole them from you.'

" ' What did you steal my horses for ? '

" ' I was tired with walking. I had been to fight the Blackfeet, and, coming back, would have called at your camp. You would have given me tobacco, but that would not carry me. When we stole them they were very poor. They are now fat. We have plenty of horses; you can take all that belong to you.' The chief then gave orders for them to deliver up all the horses taken from our camp."

Now following the Wind River to where it enters the Big Horn Mountains, Ashley detailed a

[1] See Chap. XIV.

small band to explore the canyon by water, while he, with the rest of the men and the pack train, pushed on over the range by way of Bad Pass, a distance of about thirty miles. On August 7th they reached the point where the Big Horn River issues from the mountains. Here twenty five men turned back with the horses, and, with the other twenty five, Ashley, having built bullboats for the purpose, began his voyage to the States with his precious cargo.

No difficulties were met in descending to the mouth of the Yellowstone, where the party arrived at midday on August 19th. " In effecting a landing at the junction of the two rivers," so Beckwourth informs us, " we unfortunately sunk one of our boats, on board of which were thirty packs of beaver skins, and away they went, floating down the current as rapidly as though they had been live beaver. All was noise and confusion in a moment, the General, in a perfect ferment, shouting to us to save the packs. All the swimmers plunged in after them, and every pack was saved. The noise we made attracted a strong body of U. S. troops down to the river, who were encamped near the place, and officers, privates, and musicians lined the shore. They were under the command of General Atkinson, then negotiating a treaty with the Indians of that region on behalf of the Government. General Atkinson and our General happened to be old acquaintances,

and when we had made everything snug and se-
cure, we all went into camp and freely indulged
in festivities."

It will be remembered that here, on the tongue
of land between the two rivers, Major Henry had
built a fort in the fall of 1822. After it was
abandoned a year later, the Indians set fire to it,
but Ashley found three sides of the stockade and
a part of the buildings still standing.

General Atkinson was about to start up the
Missouri for the purpose of making a treaty with
the Blackfeet, and Ashley decided to accompany
his old friend. After ascending to the mouth of
the Porcupine, and finding no Indians, the expedition returned to the mouth of the Yellowstone
within a week. Ashley now abandoned his
clumsy bullboats and transferred his cargo to a
stauncher craft furnished by General Atkinson.

On the 27th of August the combined force of
soldiers and trappers began the descent of the
Missouri, and on the 19th of September arrived
at " Council Bluffs," [1] that is to say, at Fort Atkinson. Here Ashley's party remained three
days, " which passed in continual festivities," the
trappers " feeling themselves almost at home."

Let Beckwourth finish the account of Ashley's
homeward voyage : " Providing ourselves with a
good boat, we bade adieu to the troops and con-

[1] The original Council Bluffs, so called because Lewis and
Clark there held a council with the Indians in 1804, is about 14
miles above the city of that name.

tinued our descent of the river. The current of
the Missouri is swift, but to our impatient minds
a locomotive would have seemed too tardy in
removing us from the scenes of hardship and
privation to the homes of our friends, our sweet-
hearts, our wives and little ones.

" Those who reside in maritime places, and
have witnessed the hardy tars step ashore in their
native land, can form an adequate idea of the
happy return of the mountaineers from their wanderings on the Plains to St. Louis, which is the
great seaport. Arriving at St. Charles, twenty
miles above St. Louis, the General despatched a
courier to his agents, Messrs. Warndorf and
Tracy, to inform them of his great success, and
that he would be in with his cargo the next day
about noon. When we came in sight of the city
we were saluted by a piece of artillery, which
continued its discharges until we landed at the
market place. There were not less than a thousand persons present, who hailed our landing with
shouts which deafened our ears. Those who had
parents, brothers and sisters, wives, or sweet-
hearts, met them at the landing; and such a rushing, crowding, pulling, hauling, weeping, and
laughing I had never before witnessed. Every-
one had learned of our approach by the courier.

" Our cargo was soon landed and stored, the
men receiving information that they would be paid
off that afternoon at the store of Messrs. Warn-

dorf and Tracy. We reported thither in a body to receive our pay. The full amount was counted out in silver to each man. Accordingly we all repaired to Barras's Hotel, and had a glorious time. The house was thronged with our friends besides, who all felt themselves included in the General's hospitality.

" General Ashley called on us the next morning and, perceiving that we had 'run all night,' told us to keep on another day at his expense, adding that, if we wished to indulge in a ride, he would pay for carriages. We profited by his hint, and did not fail to take into our party a good share of lasses and mountaineers. The next morning the General again visited us and, seeing we were pretty sober, paid the bill."

XVIII

GENERAL ASHLEY RETIRES

AFTER the rendezvous had broken up in July and Ashley's party had begun the journey to St. Louis with the furs, the body of trappers left behind under the command of Sublette moved leisurely up the Green River for a considerable distance. Then, having agreed upon Cache Valley as the place for the fall rendezvous, the trappers separated into small parties and spent the summer working along the streams in the country east of the Wasatch Mountains.

It was along about the end of October, 1825, and the winter was already setting in, when one of the small bands that had worked its way to the headwaters of the Salt River during the fall hunt, fell in with three men who had just arrived from St. Louis with a letter for Sublette from General Ashley. The three men were James P. Beckwourth, one La Roche, and one Pellow. It would appear that during his homeward journey Ashley had concluded that he was wealthy enough to retire, and it is probable that he had discussed with Jedediah Smith some proposition regarding the sale of his mountain interests to a new firm

of which Smith and Sublette should be members.
It was doubtless with this in view that, shortly
after arriving at St. Louis, he had induced Beckwourth and his two companions to carry a message to Sublette far away beyond the Great Divide. Beckwourth tells us that he received
$1,000 for the trip; and, considering the great
risk that so small a party ran, such remuneration
could hardly be regarded as excessive, though it
is likely that far less was received.

Setting forth from St. Louis with two riding
horses and a pack-mule for each, these three men
had followed the Missouri River to the mouth of
the Platte, ascended the latter to the Forks, thence
proceeding by way of the North Platte and the
Sweetwater through South Pass to the Green.
After pushing up the Green to the mouth of Le
Barge Creek, they had struck across country northwestward to the headwaters of the Salt River,
which empties into the Snake River where the
latter crosses the eastern boundary of Idaho.
The trappers whom they met at this point were
about to start for the rendezvous in Cache Valley, and Beckwourth decided to accompany them
to that place, there to await the arrival of Sublette rather than to search for him in the wilderness.

It was late in October when the widely scattered bands had at last reunited in Cache Valley,
and Sublette's party was the last to come in.

Upon arriving, Sublette gave orders for the whole camp to prepare for the march to the mouth of the Weber River, where he had decided to winter.   At this time the Ashley men, including hired trappers, free trappers, and those who had deserted Ogden, must have numbered about one hundred.   Most of these had taken Indian wives; some had children; and as many horses were required to transport the impedimenta of such a camp, the procession that trailed out of Cache Valley must have been rather impressive.   Joseph Meek, who became one of Sublette's trappers four years later, has left us the following account of the manner in which such a party travelled:

" When the large camp is on the march, it has a leader, generally one of the Booshways,[1] who rides in advance or at the head of the column. Near him is a led mule, chosen for qualities of speed and trustworthiness, on which are packed two small trunks that balance each other, like panniers, and which contain the company's books, papers, and articles of agreement with the men. Then follow the pack-animals, each one bearing three packs — one on each side and one on top — so nicely adjusted as not to slip in travelling. These are in charge of certain men called camp-keepers, who have each three of these to look after.   The trappers and hunters have two

[1] A corruption of the French word, *Bourgeois*, meaning trader. Sublette was the " Booshway " of the party with which we are here concerned.

horses, or mules, one to ride and one to pack their traps. If there are women and children in the train, they are all mounted. Where the country is safe, the caravan moves in single file, often stretching out for half or three-quarters of a mile. At the end of the column rides the ' second man ' or ' Little Booshway,' usually a hired officer, whose business it is to look after the order and condition of the whole camp.

" On arriving at a suitable spot upon which to make the night camp, the leader stops, dismounts in the particular space which is to be devoted to himself in its midst. The others, as they come up, form a circle, the ' second man ' bringing up the rear to be sure all are there. He then proceeds to appoint every man a place in the circle, and to examine the horses' backs to see if any are sore. The horses are then turned out, under guard, to graze; but before darkness comes on, they are placed inside the ring and picketed by a stake driven in the earth, or with two feet tied together so as to prevent easy or free locomotion. The men are divided into messes, so many trappers and so many camp-keepers to a mess. The business of eating is not a very elaborate one where the sole diet is meat, either dried or roasted. By a certain hour all is quiet in camp, and only the guard is awake.

" In the morning, at daylight, the ' second man ' comes forth from his lodge and cries in French:

'*leve, leve, leve,*' which is the command to rise. In about five minutes more he cries: '*Leche lego, leche lego,*' or ' turn out, turn out '; at which command all come out from the lodges, and the horses are turned loose to feed; but not before a horseman has galloped all around the camp at some distance, and discovered everything to be safe in the neighborhood.   Again, when the horses have been sufficiently fed under the eye of a guard, they are driven up, the packs replaced, the train mounted, and once more it moves off in the order before mentioned." [1]

Thus Ashley's men, with their women, children and horses, moved down the Bear River to Salt Lake, and along the border of the lake southward to the mouth of the Weber, where they established themselves in their skin tents for the winter.

Now that the trapping season was over, the men had a comparatively easy time, having little to do but to take turns in supplying the camp with meat and to indulge themselves in eating, sleeping, and " swapping yarns "; for we may be sure that most of the more menial duties about camp — such as cooking and fetching wood and water — were willingly performed by the squaws, as being well beneath the dignity of their lords.   Joseph Meek describes certain features of domestic economy in these winter camps:

" When a piece of game is brought in — a deer

[1] Victor.   "The River of the West."   Chap. I.

or an antelope or buffalo meat — it is thrown down in front of the Booshway's lodge; and the ' second man ' stands by and cuts it up, or has it cut up for him. The first man who chances to come along is ordered to stand still and turn his back to the pile of game, while the Little Booshway lays hold of a piece that has been cut off and asks in a loud voice: ' Who will have this? ' and the man, answering for him, says: ' The Booshway,' or perhaps ' number six ' or ' number twenty '— meaning certain messes; and the number is called to come and take the meat. In this blind way the meat is portioned out, the Booshway faring no better than his men." [1]

Not long after winter quarters had been established, so we are told by Beckwourth who was there, a party of Bannock Indians swooped down upon the camp one stormy night and drove away eighty of the white men's horses. Here was work that could not be allotted to the squaws, and such work as the trappers seemed rather to enjoy. Fifty men immediately volunteered to pursue the Bannocks; and it is safe to guess that most of those who had been on Green River in the spring of 1824 and had shared in the attack on the Snake village, were of this band which, like the former one, was led by Fitzpatrick.

Early next morning the horse-hunters set out afoot. The storm had died in the night; and, as

[1] Victor. *op. cit.* Chap. I.

much snow had fallen, the stolen herd had left a trail that was easily followed. After trudging five days in a northerly direction, the trappers came at last in sight of the Bannock village. Fitzpatrick now divided his party into two bands, one of which was led by himself, the other by the young daredevil, James Bridger, who was to drive away the Bannock horses while Fitzpatrick and his men charged the Indians, numbering about three hundred! It was surely an audacious plan, but it seems to have worked perfectly. The whole Bannock herd was driven away, though many of the horses were later recovered by the Indians. "We succeeded in getting off with the number of our own missing horses and forty head besides," says Beckwourth, who shared in the enterprise. "In the engagement six of the enemy were killed and scalped, while not one of our party received a scratch. The horses we captured were very fine ones, and our return to camp was greeted with the liveliest demonstrations."

When the horse-hunters reached winter quarters they found there an encampment of Snake Indians, numbering over a thousand. "These," so Beckwourth tells us, "had entirely surrounded us with their lodges, adding very materially to our population. They were perfectly friendly, and we apprehended no danger from them. It appears that this was their usual resort for spending the winter."

During the absence of Fitzpatrick's party, Sublette, owing, doubtless, to the letter received from Ashley, had decided that his business interests made necessary his presence in St. Louis; and he had started with but one companion, Black Harris, on the trail that led back to the States — one thousand five hundred miles away across a blizzard swept prairie-wilderness!

The wintering party, " all strong and healthy as bears," as we are assured, now settled down to a comfortable and neighborly existence in company with their Snake friends, the presence of whom made unlikely any further attack by marauding bands of horse-thieves. So passed the winter of 1825–26.

Early in the spring of 1826 four men, whose names are not recorded, set out in small bullboats from the camp at the mouth of the Weber River to skirt the shore of the Great Salt Lake. Their purpose was to locate beaver streams and to find the place whence the Buenaventura issued, flowing westward to the ocean. After three weeks these men, having circumnavigated the lake, returned to camp with a tale of unprofitable labors. They had found neither beaver nor the Buenaventura, and they had suffered much with thirst; for most of the streams that entered the lake were saline at that early season before the flood waters of the melting snow had washed them clean.

During the absence of the exploring party, the

main body had been preparing to leave winter quarters and begin the spring hunt. Many of the skins, which had been used for lodges and were therefore thoroughly cured by the smoke of the winter fires, were cut up and made into moccasins for the party. Smoked skins do not shrink with wetting as raw skins do. " This is an important quality in a moccasin," so Joseph Meek tells us, " as a trapper is almost constantly in the water during the trapping season; and should not his moccasins be smoked they will close upon his feet, in drying, like a vice. Sometimes after trapping all day, the tired and soaked trapper lies down in his blankets at night, still wet. By and by he is wakened by the pinching of his moccasins and is obliged to rise and seek the water again to relieve himself of the pain. For the same reason, when the spring comes, the trapper is forced to cut off the lower half of his buckskin breeches, and piece them down with blanket leggings, which he wears all through the trapping season." [1]

The whole body of trappers and Indians now broke camp and moved together up Bear River to Cache Valley, where forty five packs of beaver, collected during the previous fall, were cached. During this operation, two French Canadian trappers were killed by the caving in of a clay bank in which they were digging; and Beckwourth, with his usual loquacity, tells us that he fell heir to the

[1] Victor. *op. cit.*

widow of one of these unfortunates. " She was
of light complexion," says he, " smart, trim, and
active, and never tired in her efforts to please me,
seeming to think that she belonged to me for the
remainder of her life. I had never had a servant
before, and I found her of great service to me in
keeping my clothes in repair, making my bed, and
taking care of my weapons."

From Cache Valley, the trappers started on the
spring hunt, pushing over to the headwaters of the
Port Neuf and down that stream to its junction
with the Snake River, finding plenty of beaver all
the way. At this point they seem to have had
a brisk encounter with a large band of Blackfeet,
as a result of which they lost three horses. However, they took some scalps by way of partial
remuneration! They then turned back, ascending the Port Neuf to its headwaters, from whence
they crossed over to the Bear River, continuing
the hunt along that stream and its tributaries
until they reached the mouth of Sage Creek.
There they met Black Harris and one Porteleuse,
who had just arrived from the States. These
brought the news that Ashley, Smith, and Sublette were but a short distance away, bound for
Salt Lake with fifty men and a pack-train of one
hundred horses and mules, having begun the journey from St. Louis early in March.

Upon receiving this news, the trappers hastened
back to Salt Lake, being joined on the way by the

Snake Indians who had spent the previous winter with them. Shortly after they reached the appointed place of rendezvous on Salt Lake, Ashley's party came in with the pack-train heavily laden with merchandise, and the business of the rendezvous began.

"It may well be supposed," so Beckwourth remarks, "that the arrival of such a vast amount of luxuries from the East did not pass off without a general celebration. Mirth, songs, dancing, shouting, trading, running, jumping, racing, target-shooting, yarns, frolic, with all sorts of extravagances that white men or Indians could invent, were freely indulged in. The unpacking of the medicine water (alcohol) contributed not a little to the heightening of our festivities."

However, the festivities were rudely interrupted during the second day, when a body of Blackfeet, prowling in the vicinity, surprised and killed five of the Snake Indians who were gathering roots at some distance from the camp. Whereupon the Snake chief went to Sublette and said: "Cut Face, three of my warriors and two women have just been killed by the Blackfeet. You say that your warriors can fight — that they are great braves. Now let me see them fight, that I may know your words are true."

Sublette replied: "You shall see them fight, and then you will know that they are all braves — that I have no cowards among my men, and that they are all ready to die for their Snake friends."

Beckwourth, whom we have been quoting, tells us that the ensuing battle continued for six hours, after which Sublette's men, having become very hungry as a result of their violent exercise, retired to their camp, requesting that the Snakes remain on the field and finish the job. But the Snakes, it seems, had also developed considerable appetites by this time, and, concluding that under the circumstances they would rather eat than fight, they followed their allies to the feast. So the battle ended pleasantly enough.

During the rendezvous General Ashley completed arrangements with Jedediah Smith, David E. Jackson, and William L. Sublette, whereby he transferred his interests in the mountains to the firm of Smith, Jackson and Sublette, agreeing to furnish the new company with goods from the States and to dispose of its furs on a commission basis. The articles of agreement were drawn up and signed on July 26th, 1826, "near the Grand Lake west of the Rocky Mountains."

Before leaving the country for the last time, so Beckwourth informs us, the General delivered the following farewell address: "Mountaineers and friends! When I first came to the mountains, I came a poor man. You, by your indefatigable exertions, toils, and privations, have procured me an independent fortune. With ordinary prudence in the management of what I have accumulated, I shall never want for anything.   For this, my friends, I feel myself under great obligations to you.   Many of you have served with me personally, and I shall always be proud to testify to the fidelity with which you have stood by me through all danger, and the friendly and brotherly manner which you have ever, one and all, evinced toward me.   For these faithful and devoted services I wish you to accept my thanks; the gratitude I express to you springs from my heart, and will ever retain a lively hold on my feelings.   My friends!   I am now about to leave you to take up my abode in St. Louis.   Whenever any of you return thither, your first duty must be to call at my house, to talk over the scenes of peril we have encountered, and partake of the best cheer my table can afford.   I now wash my hands of the toils of the Rocky Mountains.   Farewell, mountaineers and friends!   May God bless you all!" [1]

[1] While quoting James P. Beckwourth rather freely in the foregoing pages, I have not been unaware of the fact that some of our earlier historians of the West have been inclined to regard him as unreliable. However that may be, he is certainly important for his intimate descriptions of well authenticated incidents. It is as a describer of such incidents that I have trusted him.— Author.

XIX

THE FIRST AMERICANS OVERLAND TO CALIFORNIA [1]

IMMEDIATELY upon taking over Ashley's interests in the mountains, Smith, Jackson and Sublette began to make plans for extending the business. The country drained by the Green, the Bear, the Weber, and the upper Snake rivers, was still rich in beaver; but yonder between the Great Salt Lake and the setting sun lay a land unknown. What incalculable wealth of fur might be waiting there in a trapper's paradise of pleasant valleys! And somewhere through that country did not the mighty Buenaventura River flow westward to the Pacific? Here was stuff enough for the fashioning of big dreams! Beyond that unknown land was California. Might it not be possible to transport furs to some Spanish port, thence to be sent around the Horn by the New England trading ships that were constantly on the coast in those years?

It will be remembered that in the late fall of 1824 Jedediah Smith had accompanied Ross to Flathead House, the Hudson Bay Company's post

[1] This chapter is based on Smith's letter to General Clark (Kansas Hist. Soc. MSS.) and the Journals of Harrison G. Rogers (Missouri Hist. Soc. MSS.); both presented in full by Dale, the latter for the first time.

on Clark's Fork of the Columbia east of the Bitter
Root Mountains.   While there he had learned
much regarding the successful operations of the
British traders, and he could not have failed to
appreciate the immense advantage they enjoyed
with their access to the sea by way of the Columbia.   It was natural that the young Americans
should covet a like advantage, especially as the
memory of Astor's great enterprise, that had
failed but twelve years before, was fresh in their
minds and still bore the glamour of high adventure.

Might not the Buenaventura prove to be a
second Columbia?

It was decided that an exploring party should
be sent through the unknown country to the sea.
Three years had passed since Jedediah Smith, who
was now just twenty eight years old, had joined
Ashley's band at St. Louis, and from the beginning he had been a man of mark.   His conduct in
the first battle with the Rees and his perilous
journey afterward to Major Henry at the mouth
of the Yellowstone, had distinguished him for ex-
traordinary courage; and since that time he had
demonstrated shrewdness in business matters,
commonsense, and a gift for leadership.   For
these reasons, and because, being better educated
than either of his comrades, he was the best fitted
to deal with the Spanish authorities on the coast,
it was decided that he should lead the exploring
party.

We can fancy with what eagerness he must have accepted this task; for had he not pored over that vast triangular white space on the maps of the period and dreamed of penetrating its mystery? Now the dream was coming true! However, judging by the direction he took on his outward journey, it would seem that his first concern was with finding a practicable route to California.

On the 22nd of August, 1826, Smith started southward from the place of rendezvous on Great Salt Lake with fifteen men, fifty horses, and a stock of merchandise, leaving his partners, Jackson and Sublette, with the remainder of the band to continue operations in the fur country already explored, and agreeing to meet them, if possible, at the southern end of Bear Lake during the summer of 1827. Those who accompanied Smith are worthy of remembrance, for they were the first Americans to reach California by land, the vanguard of the great invasion that was to be in full swing a quarter of a century later. Their names are as follows: Harrison G. Rogers, Silas Gobel, Arthur Black, John Gaiter, Robert Evans, Manuel Lazarus, John Hanna, John Wilson, Martin McCoy, Daniel Ferguson, Peter Ranne (a negro), Abraham LaPlant, James Read, John Reubasco, and one Robiseau.

Following the valley of the Jordan River from Great Salt Lake, Smith's party skirted the eastern shore of Utah Lake. Having reached the

point where the lake shore bears westward, they
struck out across the barren country to the southwest, and early in September came upon the
Sevier River, flowing in a northerly direction.
Smith called this Ashley's River, and assumed that
it emptied into Utah Lake — a natural assump-
tion, considering the direction of the stream and
the fact that he reached it at a considerable distance south of the abrupt bend from which it flows
southwestwardly into Sevier Lake. Just fifty
years before, the two Franciscan padres, Domin-
guez and Escalante, in their misguided search for
a direct route from Santa Fé to Monterey, had
passed that way with a party of eight *en route*
to Utah Lake. Since then no white man had penetrated that solitude until now.

Smith's band pushed on southward up the valley of the Sevier. The last signs of buffalo had
been seen before leaving Utah Lake, but antelope
and mountain sheep were still to be found in small
numbers, and " black-tailed hares " were abundant, so that the men as yet did not suffer want.
While ascending this stream, they came upon a
small village of Sanpet Indians, called Sanpatch
by Smith. The fact that these wore " rabbit skin
robes " is sufficient indication that big game was
very scarce in that region. Few in numbers and
poverty-stricken, it is not surprising that this tribe
was " friendly disposed " toward the white men,
who must have seemed immensely rich and pow-

erful with their buckskin clothes, their rifles, and their pack-animals laden with merchandise.

From the headwaters of the Sevier, the explorers crossed the divide southward and, near the end of September, reached the headwaters of the Virgin ("of a muddy cast and a little brackish"), which Smith called "Adams' River in compliment to our President." With mountains to their left and a sandy waste, broken by occasional rocky hills, on their right, they descended the Virgin through a country where even jackrabbits were scarce. They now began to know hunger, and their horses grew lean and weak for want of grass. Nor did their meeting with the Paiute Indians bring them much relief. These, like the Sanpets on the Sevier, wore rabbit skin robes and were poor, though we are told that they "raised some little corn and pumpkins."

After ten days of marching down the Virgin, so Smith tells us, he discovered a large cave on the west side of the river, "the entrance of which is about ten or fifteen feet high and five or six feet in width," the roof, sides, and floor being solid rock salt. Two days farther down stream, through a region where little grew but cacti and stunted shrubs, they reached the point where the Virgin empties into the Colorado. Crossing the Colorado, which Smith calls the Seedskeeder (Siskadee), thus identifying it with Green River, the band travelled down the valley four days, finding

the country " remarkably barren, rocky, and mountainous." We are not told how they managed
to exist during this time, but it is reasonable to
assume that they lived on horse meat.

At length they came upon the Mohave Indians
(whom Smith calls the Ammuchabas), dwelling
in a place where the valley, opening out to a width
of from five to fifteen miles, was well timbered
and fertile. The Mohaves were well supplied
with corn, beans, pumpkins, watermelons, and
wheat.

" I was now nearly destitute of horses," says
Smith, " and had learned what it was to do without food. I therefore remained there fifteen days
and recruited my men, and I was enabled also to
exchange my horses and purchase a few more of
a few runaway Indians who stole some from the
Spaniards. I here got information of the Spanish countries (the Californias), obtained two
good guides, and recrossed the Seedskeeder which
I afterwards found emptied into the Gulf of California by the name of the Collarado."

Having crossed the Colorado at the Needles
during the first week of November, Smith and his
band struck out across the desert. " I travelled
a west course fifteen days," he says, " over a country of complete barrens, generally travelling from
morning until night without water. I crossed a
salt plain about twenty miles long and eight wide;
on the surface was a crust of beautiful white salt,

quite thin. Under this surface there is a layer of salt from a half to one and one-half inches in depth; between this and the upper layer there is about four inches of yellowish sand."

Anyone who has crossed the Mohave Desert on the Atchison, Topeka and Santa Fé Railroad, the route of which is approximately that followed by Smith, can easily imagine what hardships were suffered by this party. They had started from Great Salt Lake with fifty horses; and though they had purchased a number while resting among the Mohave Indians, they had but eighteen when they reached the Spanish settlements of California. Some had doubtless been eaten, but most had died for want of pasturage and water.

On Sunday evening, November 26th, 1826, Smith's party encamped at a point about eighteen miles east of San Gabriel Mission situated near the Pueblo of Los Angeles. The next morning, so says Harrison G. Rogers in his journal, " We got ready as early as possible and started a west course and travelled fourteen miles and encamped for the day. We passed innumerable herds of cattle, horses, and some hundreds of sheep. We passed four or five Indian lodges, that their Indians act as herdsmen. There came an old Indian to us that speaks good Spanish, and took us with him to his mansion, which consisted of two rows of large and lengthy buildings, that remind me of the British Barracks. So soon as we encamped, there was plenty prepared to eat, a fine young cow killed, and a plenty of corn meal given us. Pretty soon after, the two commandants of the missionary establishment (San Gabriel) came to us and had the appearance of gentlemen. Mr. Smith went with them to the Mansion (Mission) and I stayed with the company. There was great feasting among the men as they were pretty hungry, not having any good meat for some time."

The next day, so Rogers continues, " Mr. Smith wrote me that he was received as a gentleman and treated as such, and that he wished me to go back and look for a pistol that was lost, and send the company on to the missionary establishment. I complied with his request, went back, and found the pistol, and arrived late in the evening. Was received very politely, and showed into a room and my arms taken from me. About ten o'clock at night supper was served, and Mr. Smith and myself sent for. I was introduced to the two priests over a glass of good old whisky and found them to be very jovial friendly gentlemen. The supper consisted of a number of different dishes, served different from any table I ever saw. Plenty of good wine during supper. Before the cloth was removed cigars were introduced."

It was a strange society into which these American trappers had come — almost like men from another planet. Their trail from St. Louis up the Missouri, the Platte and the Sweetwater,

through South Pass to Salt Lake by way of the
Bear River, past Utah Lake, up the Sevier, down
the Virgin and Colorado, and westward across the
Mohave Desert, had led them far as to space,
but farther as to time; for they had actually jour-
neyed backward through the Past of the Race, to
a pastoral, theocratic age!

At this point, a brief sketch of early California
history may not come amiss. In 1543, Juan Cab-
rillo, a Spanish navigator, had explored the southern coast of Upper California, then, and for many
years thereafter, supposed to be an island or an
archipelago with an extension of the Gulf of California on the east and the mythical Strait of
Anian (an arm of Hudson Bay!) on the north.
In the 80's and 90's of the same century, two
Spanish galleons, trading with the Philippines
from the west coast of Mexico, had touched upon
the California shore; and in 1602 Sebastian Vis-
caino had discovered the bays of San Diego and
Monterey. For over a century and a half thereafter, the country, though regarded as belonging
to the Spanish crown, was unvisited, and remained
little more than a name associated with the
" Northern Mystery." Now and then a galleon,
homeward bound from the Philippines, sighted its
lonely headlands afar and sailed on.

In the middle of the 18th century the Russians
began the exploration of Alaska, and Spain, fear-
ing the new influence growing up in the far North,

alarmed at the increasing frequency with which
the English privateers were appearing in the Pacific, and having long felt the need of a refitting
port for her Manila galleons, was aroused to a
new interest in the land that she had so long neglected, and decided to occupy it.

At this time, however, the Spanish Government was too poor to undertake the conquest of
the vast domain by force of arms; and so the task
was delegated to the Franciscan Order of missionary friars. I. B. Richman remarks upon
" the singular efficacy of the Cross in the subjuga-
tion of men," [1] a fact which the Spanish religious
orders had already demonstrated in the Philippine
Islands, Paraguay, and Lower California. The
leader of the great movement which now began
was the famous Father Junípero Serra. In 1768
he accompanied the " sacred expedition " under
José de Galvez, the purpose of which was to establish missions at certain strategic points along the
California coast. The first, San Diego de Alcalá,
was founded in July, 1769; the second, San Carlos
Borromeo, near the present Monterey, in 1770;
the third San Antonio de Padua, on the San Antonio River, in July, 1771; and San Gabriel Arc-
angel, the fourth, in September of the same year.
From that time on, the movement had grown rapidly. At the time of Jedediah Smith's arrival,
there were twenty three thriving missions in Up-

[1] " California Under Spain and Mexico."

per California, reaching from the Bay of San Francisco to San Diego Bay. Of these, San Gabriel was one of the most important, owing to the fertility of the region and to the fact that there the overland route from the Colorado River met the trail from Lower California.

In spite of the undeniably pious intentions of the padres, these missions had grown to be something more than religious institutions, concerned with the salvation of the Indian soul. They were commercial concerns, under theocratic control and flourishing by virtue of a practically unlimited supply of slave labor. The Indian neophytes tended the flocks and herds, spun wool, tanned hides, made tallow and soap, raised wheat, hemp, grapes, olives, oranges, and manufactured various articles in leather, wood, and iron. A profitable trade in hides and tallow had, for many years, been carried on with the Boston ships that came around the Horn — a voyage that often required as much as six months to make. R. H. Dana, in " Two Years Before the Mast," has left us a vivid account of that industry as it was carried on along the coast during the period with which we are concerned.

Four years before Smith's arrival, the Province of Upper California had given allegiance to Mexico, which had broken away from Spain in 1811.

Now the cordial reception of the first overland Americans by the benevolent and lovable padres of San Gabriel Mission proved to be somewhat misleading; for there was another power in the country with which the party was obliged to reckon — the civil authorities.   As we have seen, the first settlements in California had been founded as the result of suspicion and fear — suspicion of the Russians, fear of the British buccaneers of the type of Hawkins and Drake.   Since the ship *Otter* of Boston had dropped anchor in the Bay of Monterey just thirty years before, the Americans had come to be regarded with some dread; and not without cause, as history has long since made plain, and as the conduct of the Boston smugglers and traders along the coast had then already demonstrated.   We Americans are a virile, driving breed; and we must have seemed rather grasping and godless to the ease-loving Spaniards of the Coast in those days.   Why had these barbaric trappers from the central wilds of the continent entered California?   Was a new race of Goths looking lustfully upon a new Italy?

Immediately upon arriving at San Gabriel, Smith was informed that he could not proceed without a passport from the civil authorities, and accordingly he wrote a letter to the Governor of the Province, José Maria de Echeandía, whose official residence was then at San Diego, giving reasons for his presence in the country and asking permission to continue his journey northward. Smith's reasons seem to have been rather more strategic than factual, and considering those with whom he had to deal, he was doubtless justified in making them so. The Governor was given to understand that the party had been " compelled for want of provisions and water " to enter California. Though an answer was expected within a few days, more than a month was to elapse before satisfactory arrangements could be made with Echeandía; and, knowing this, we may as well pass the time among the luxury-loving padres with Harrison G. Rogers. Here follow extracts from his diary:

" November 29th. Still at the mansion (Mission). We were sent for about sunrise to drink a cup of tea, and eat some bread and cheese. They all appear friendly and treat us well. Although they are Catholics by profession, they allow us the liberty of conscience, and treat us as they do their own countrymen and brethren.

" About eleven o'clock dinner was ready, and the priest came after us to go and dine. We were invited into the office and invited to take a glass of gin and water and eat some bread and cheese. Directly after, we were seated at dinner, and everything went on in style, both the priests being pretty merry, the clerk and one other gentleman who speaks some English. They all appear to be gentlemen of the first class, both in manners and habits. The Mission consists of four rows of houses forming a complete square, where there are all kinds of mechanics at work. The church faces the east, and the guard house, the west. The north and south line comprises the work shops. They have large vineyards, apple and peach orchards, and some orange and some fig trees. They manufacture blankets and sundry other articles. They distil whisky and grind their own grain, having a water mill of a tolerable quality. They have upwards of one thousand persons employed, men, women, and children, Indians of various nations. The situation is very handsome, pretty streams of water running through from all quarters, some thousands of acres of fertile land, as level as a die in view, and a part under cultivation, surrounded on the north with a high mountain, handsomely timbered with pine and cedar, and on the south with low mountains covered with grass. Cattle — this Mission has upwards of thirty thousand head of cattle, and horses, sheep, hogs, etc. in proportion. . . . They slaughter at this place from two to three thousand head of cattle at a time. The Mission lives on the profits.

"November 30th. There was a wedding in this place today, and Mr. Smith and myself invited. The bell was rung a little before sunrise, and the morning service performed. Then the music commenced serenading, the soldiers firing, etc. About seven o'clock tea and bread served, and about eleven, dinner and music. The ceremony and dinner were held at the priest's. They had an elegant dinner, consisting of a number of dishes, boiled and roast meat and fowl, wine and brandy, grapes brought as a dessert. Mr. Smith and myself acted quite independent, not understanding their language, nor they ours. We endeavored to apologize, being very dirty and not in a situation to shift our clothing; but no excuse would be taken. They treat us as gentlemen in every sense of the word; and although our apparel is so indifferent, and we not being in circumstances at this time to help ourselves, being about eight hundred miles on a direct line from the place of our deposit. . . . Our two Indian guides were imprisoned in the guard house the second day after we arrived at the missionary establishment, and remain confined as yet.

"December 1st, 1826. We still remain at the Mission of San Gabriel; things going on as usual; all friendship and peace. Mr. Smith set his blacksmiths, James Reed and Silas Gobel, to work in the blacksmith shop to make a bear trap for the priest, agreeable to promise yesterday. Mr. Smith and the interpreter went in the evening to the next Mission, called St. Pedro (on San Pedro Bay), a Spanish gentleman from the Mission having sent his servant with horses for them. . . . Mr. Smith informed me this morning that he had to give Reed a little flogging yesterday evening on account of some impertinence. He appeared more complaisant this morning than usual.

" December 2nd. . . . Mr. Smith has not returned from the Mission as yet. This province is called the Province of New California. This mission ships annually from twenty to twenty five thousand dollars worth of hides and tallow, and about twenty thousand dollars worth of soap. . . . The Indians appear to be much altered from the wild Indians in the mountains that we have passed. They are kept in great fear. For the least offence they are corrected. They are complete slaves in every sense of the word. . . . Mr. Smith and La Plant returned late in the evening, and represent their treatment to be good at the other Mission. Mr. Smith tells me that Mr. Francisco, the Spanish gentleman that he went to visit, promises him as many horses and mules as he wants.

" December 4th. Still at San Gabriel; things much as usual. The priest presented Mr. Smith with two pieces of shirting containing sixty four yards, for to make the men shirts, all being nearly naked.

" December 7th. No answer as yet from the Governor of the Province. Mr. Smith and all hands getting impatient. . . .

" December 8th. Mr. Smith was sent for, to go to San Diego to see the Governor. Captain Cunningham, commanding the ship *Courier,* now lying in port at San Diego, arrived here late this evening. The Captain is a Bostonian and has been trading on the coast for hides and tallow since June last. He informs me that he is rather under the impression that he shall be obliged to remain until some time in the succeeding summer, in consequence of so much opposition, as there are a number of vessels on the coast trading for the same articles. . . . Mr. Martinas tells me that there are between sixteen and seventeen thousand natives that are converted to the Catholic faith and under the control of the different missions. The white population he estimates at six thousand, making twenty two or twenty three thousand souls in the Province of New California.

" December 9th. Mr. Smith and one of the men, in company with Captain Cunningham, left San Gabriel this morning for San Diego, the Governor's place of residence. . . .

" December 10th, Sunday. There were five Indians brought to the Mission and sentenced to be whipped for not going to work when ordered. Each received from twelve to fourteen lashes. They were all old men, say from fifty to sixty years, the commandant standing by with his sword to see that the Indian who flogged them did his duty. . . . They keep at this place four small field pieces, two six-pounders and two two-pounders, to protect them from the Indians in case they should rebel.

" December 13th. I walked through the workshops. I saw some Indians blacksmithing, some carpentering, others making the woodwork of plows, others employed in making spinning wheels for the squaws to spin on.   There are upwards of sixty women employed in spinning yarn and weaving. . . . Our blacksmiths have been employed for several days making horse shoes and nails for our own use when we leave here.

"December 14th.   I was asked by the priest to let our blacksmiths make a large trap for him to set in his orange garden to catch the Indians when they come up at night to rob his orchard.

"December 18th.   I received a letter from Mr. Smith informing me that he was rather under the impression that he would be detained for some time yet, as the general did not like to take the responsibility on himself to let us pass, until he received instructions from the general in Mexico. . . . Our men have been employed in fitting out a cargo of hides, tallow and soap for a Mr. Henry Edwards.   He is what they call here a Mexican trader.

"December 19th.   This mission, if properly managed, would be equal to a mine of silver or gold.   Their farms are extensive.   They raise from three thousand to four thousand bushels of wheat annually, and sell to shippers for three dollars per bushel.   The annual income, situated as it is and managed so badly by the Indians, is worth, in hides, tallow, soap, wine, brandy, wheat, and corn, from fifty five to sixty thousand dollars.

" December 20th. I expect an answer from Mr. Smith in six or eight days if he does not get permission to pass on. My situation is a very delicate one, as I have to be among the grandees of the country every day. . . . I make a very grotesque appearance when seated at table amongst the dandies with their ruffles, silks, and broad clothes. . . .

" January 6th, 1827. This being what is called Epiphany, or Old Christmas Day. . . . Church held early as usual, men, women, and children attend. After church the ceremonies as on Sundays. Wine issued abundantly to both Spaniards and Indians, music played by the Indian band. After the issue of the morning, our men, in company with some Spaniards, went and fired a salute, and the old Padre gave them wine, bread, and meat as a treat. Some of the men got drunk and two of them, James Reed and Daniel Ferguson, commenced fighting, and some of the Spaniards interfered and struck one of our men by the name of Black, which came very near terminating with bad consequences. . . . Our blacksmith, James Reed, came very abruptly into the priest's dining room while at dinner, and asked for brandy. The priest ordered a plate of victuals to be handed to him. He ate a few mouthfuls, and set the plate on the table, and then took up the decanter of wine and drank without invitation, and came very near breaking the glass when he set it down.

The Padre, seeing he was in a state of inebriety, refrained from saying anything. . . .

"Monday, January 8th.   Last night there was a great fandango or dance among the Spaniards. They kept it up till nearly daylight. . . .

"Wednesday, January 10th.   About noon Mr. Smith, Captain Cunningham, Mr. Shaw, and Thomas Dodge came to the Mission from the ship *Courier,* and I was much rejoiced to see them, as I have been waiting with anxiety to see him. . . ."

So runs a portion of the diary of Harrison G. Rogers — a Western Pepys.

After weeks of trying negotiations with the suspicious and procrastinating authorities, Smith, with the aid of Captain Cunningham and several other New England seamen then on the coast, managed to get permission to proceed on his way. From San Diego he sailed to the port of San Pedro on board the *Courier* with Captain Cunningham; and by the middle of January, 1827, we find him at the Pueblo of Los Angeles engaged in buying horses for his journey.

On the 16th of January Smith returned to the Mission from the Pueblo with the horses he had purchased there.   During the following day preparations were made for resuming the journey, and old Father Sanchez, who had already given much to the visitors, outdid himself in generosity. When the band was ready to start, Daniel Ferguson, who was evidently well pleased with Southern California and had no desire to experience any further hardships in the wilderness, could not be found. John Wilson also remained at San Gabriel, probably by arrangement with Smith.

On the 18th of January, 1827, the party, now consisting of fourteen men, including Smith, set out northwestward with sixty eight horses which, being for the most part unbroken, soon became unmanageable and ran " eight or ten miles " with the packs before they could be stopped. Camp was made that night at the Indian farmhouse where the party had passed the night of November 27th, 1826, and Smith and Rogers returned to the Mission for a farewell supper with the friendly padres.

Travelling in a northeasterly direction for the next two days, they made camp within four miles of San Bernardino, " where," says Rogers, " we have an order from the Governor and our old Father Joseph Sanchez for all the supplies we stand in need of." Here some days were spent in purchasing provisions, drying meat, making pack-saddles, breaking horses, and in rounding up the troublesome herd which broke away several times.

Thence pushing on in a northwesterly direction up the great central valley for a distance of about three hundred miles, in early spring the party reached a river which Smith called the Wim-

mulche, after a tribe of Indians found there.
Authorities differ as to the identity of this stream,
Chittenden [1] believing it to be the Merced, and
Richman,[2] the Mokelumnes; but Dale [3] gives what
seem to be conclusive arguments in favor of the
Stanislaus.

Smith, eager to reach the place of rendezvous
agreed upon with Jackson and Sublette, now un-
dertook to cross the Sierras. His chosen route,
which is not definitely known, probably ran
twenty five or thirty miles north of the Yosemite
Valley. " I found the snow so deep on Mount
Joseph," he wrote to General Clark, " that I
could not cross my horses, five of which starved to
death. I was compelled, therefore, to return to
the valley which I had left, and there, leaving my
party, I started with two men, seven horses and
two mules and provisions for ourselves, and
started on the 20th of May, and succeeded in
crossing it in eight days, having lost only two
horses and one mule. I found the snow on the
top of this mountain from four to eight feet deep,
but it was so consolidated by the heat of the sun
that my horses only sunk from half a foot to one
foot deep."

One of the men who accompanied Smith is
known to have been the blacksmith, Silas Gobel.

[1] " History of the American Fur Trade." Page 284 and Map.
[2] " California Under Spain and Mexico." Map of the Southwest.
[3] " Ashley-Smith Explorations." Page 192.

His other companion is nowhere named as such. However, by collating the lists of those who are known to have been, or must have been, in the parties of 1826, 1827, and 1828, it appears that Smith's other companion could have been no other than Robiseau.

" After travelling twenty days from the east side of Mount Joseph," continues Smith's letter, " I struck the southwest corner of Great Salt Lake, travelling over a country completely barren and destitute of game. We frequently travelled without water, sometimes for two days over sandy deserts where there was no sign of vegetation, and when we found water in some of the rocky hills, we most generally found some Indians who appeared the most miserable of the human race, having nothing to subsist on (nor any clothing) except grass-seed, grasshoppers, etc. When we arrived at the Salt Lake, we had but one horse and one mule remaining, which were so feeble and poor that they could scarce carry the little camp equipage which I had along; the balance of my horses I was compelled to eat as they gave out."

Thus characteristically, with few words, Smith describes what was unquestionably a great feat and what must have been a terrible experience. Twenty days of toil and suffering in an unknown desert, and all summed up in one hundred fifty words! Most men would require more space for the discussion of an aching tooth.

With two companions Smith had at last penetrated the great triangular white space of his
dream.   He had found no pleasant valleys rich
in beaver; but he had been the first to travel the
central route between the Great Salt Lake and
the Pacific Ocean.   The road from the Missouri
River to San Francisco Bay was now open, await-
ing the wagons of the settlers — and the official
explorers!

XX

SMITH'S SECOND JOURNEY [1]

ON about the 17th of June, 1827, Jedediah
Smith and his two companions, having
crossed the Nevada deserts, reached the southern
end of Salt Lake, from whence they hastened on
to the southern end of Bear Lake, the place
chosen by the three partners for the summer
rendezvous. On July 17th, we find Smith still
at the Bear Lake rendezvous, writing a brief account of his recent journey to the Superintendent
of Indian Affairs, General William Clark.
Shortly thereafter his second journey to California began. His party consisted of nineteen
men and two Indian women. The names of the
men are as follows: Thomas Virgin (for whom
the Virgin River was named), Charles Swift,
Toussaint Marishall, John Turner, Joseph Palmer, Joseph La Point, Thomas Daws, Richard
Taylor, Silas Gobel, David Cunningham, Francis
Deramme, William Campbell, Boatswain Brown,

[1] This chapter is based on a MS. of the Kansas Hist. Soc.,
entitled, "Brief account of accidents, misfortunes, and depreda-
tions committed by Indians on the firm of Smith, Jackson and
Sublette, since July 1, 1826, to the present, 1829"; and on the
Rogers Journals.

Gregory Ortaga, John B. Ratelle, Pale, Polite, Robiseau, Isaac Galbraith.

Following the same route that he had taken the year before, in late August Smith reached the country of the Mohave Indians near the point where the 35th parallel crosses the Colorado River. It will be remembered that Smith spent fifteen days with the Mohaves on his way to California the year before. Having good reason to regard them as friendly, he decided to spend a few days among them now, resting his men and horses and purchasing supplies before beginning the difficult westward journey across the desert. He could not know that, during the past year, these Indians had been ordered by Governor Echeandía to stop any Americans who might attempt to pass that way.

After spending three days in peaceful trade with the Mohaves, Smith prepared to resume his journey. As on his previous trip, he had crossed the Colorado some distance above, and was now on the east side of the river. Unconscious of treacherous intent on the part of his hosts, he went about the task of transporting his party to the west bank by means of rafts made of bundles of reeds, the Indians very obligingly lending a hand. Smith and nine of his men had already crossed, some of the party was still on the east shore, and the remainder on the raft in mid-stream, when, at a signal, the Mohaves fell upon their departing guests. The two Indian women were taken captive, Thomas Virgin was seriously wounded, and the following ten, who had not yet reached the west bank, were massacred: Gobel, Cunningham, Deramme, Campbell, Brown, Ortaga, Ratelle, Pale, Polite, and Robiseau. All of Smith's property and papers were lost.

There was nothing for the survivors to do but to flee into the desert to the west. Travelling both by night and by day, they reached the Spanish settlements near San Gabriel Mission in nine and one-half days. Considering the fact that Smith had spent fifteen days in covering the same ground on his former trip, one can imagine the mood of desperation that drove him now.

Immediately upon arriving at the settlements, Smith reported by letter to the proper authorities; and, having purchased some supplies (for the party was destitute), he pushed on northwestwardly up the central valley to join the band of eleven men that he had left in the region of the Stanislaus River on his departure for Salt Lake in May of that year. During the absence of their leader, the little band had fared badly, and Smith found them half starved. He and his companions were no better off; and there was nothing to do but to place himself once more at the doubtful mercy of the Spaniards. So, with two Indian guides, Smith went to the Mission of San José — a three days' journey. There he made his wants known and asked permission to go on to Monterey where Governor Echeandía was then residing. He was arrested and thrown into a guard house, from which, however, he was allowed to write to the Captain of the Upper Province.

About two weeks passed before he received a letter from the Governor, inviting him to call. Then, disarmed and guarded by four soldiers, he set out for Monterey, where he arrived at midnight after a journey of three days. Again he was thrown into prison, remaining there without food or water until the following noon, when the Governor sent for him.

As a result of the first interview, Smith " obtained liberty of the limits of the town and harbor and of boarding with an American gentleman (Captain Cooper) of Boston." Day after day passed by, and still Echeandía could not make up his mind as to what should be done with this American trapper who had actually committed the crime of entering Mexican territory! At times it seemed that the intruder would be sent to Mexico; again, he must leave the country by ship; at other times, the whole party yonder in the region of the Stanislaus was to be summoned to Monterey.

Finally, when it became apparent that the Governor was quite incapable of a decision, four American sea captains, whose vessels were lying in the harbor, took the matter into their own hands and appointed Captain Cooper agent for the United States. Cooper soon settled the matter, and on November 15th, 1827, Smith gave bond in the sum of thirty thousand dollars, promising to leave the country within two months.

Smith had left nineteen men encamped in the region of the Stanislaus when he went to Monterey; and during his tedious negotiations with the Governor, these had been brought into San Francisco, where Smith now joined them after purchasing some horses, guns, ammunition and other necessities. Thomas Virgin, who had been left in the South because of his wounds, was sent for. At about this time two of the men, who seem to have been Isaac Galbraith and the quarrelsome blacksmith, James Read, deserted, leaving the following nineteen in the band that began the return journey early in December: Smith, Rogers, Virgin, Black, La Point, Daws, La Plant, Swift, Turner, Gaiter, Hanna, Lazarus, Palmer, Ranne (the negro), Taylor, McCoy, Reubasco, Marishall, and Evans.

Trapping as they went, these moved slowly up the Sacramento River, spending considerable time on the largest tributary of that stream, which, for that reason, has since been called American Fork. It seems to have been Smith's intention to cross the Sierras as early in the spring as possible, and return to Salt Lake through the unknown country lying north of his route of 1827.

But in April, 1828, after several unsuccessful attempts to find a practicable pass to the eastward, he was forced to change his plan and make for the Columbia. He now left the Sacramento Valley, striking out through the mountainous country in the direction of the coast.

By the 13th of May, 1828, he had crossed the Trinity River near latitude 40° 30′, and reached the base of Hoopa Mountain. The following extracts from the Journal kept by Rogers during this time will give some idea of the difficulties encountered by the party:

"Wednesday, May 14th. We made an early start, directing our course northwest, and travelled four miles and encamped on the top of a high mountain, where there was but indifferent grass for the horses. The travelling amazing bad; we descended one point of brushy and rocky mountain where it took us about six hours to get the horses down, some of them falling about fifty feet perpendicular down a steep place into a creek. One broke his neck. A number of packs left along the trail, as night was fast approaching, and we were obliged to leave them and get what horses we could, collected at camp. A number more got badly hurt by the falls, but none killed but this one that broke his neck. Saw some Indians (Hoopas) that crossed the river in a canoe and came to see us. . . . They appear afraid of horses. They are very light-colored Indians, quite small and talkative.

" Thursday, 15th May, 1828. The men were divided into parties this morning, some sent hunting, as we have no meat in camp, others sent back for the horses.

" Friday, May 16th, 1828. We concluded that it was best to lie by today and send two men to look out a pass to travel, as the country looks awful ahead, and let our horses rest, as there is pretty good grass about one mile off for them to feed on. . . .

" Saturday, May 17th. The two men that were sent on discovery yesterday returned this morning, and say that we are fifteen or twenty miles from the North Pacific Ocean. They report game plenty, such as elk and deer. They report the travelling favorable to what it has been for thirty or forty miles back. . . . The two men, Marishall and Turner, that were sent off yesterday, killed three deer, and Captain Smith has dispatched two men after the meat, as the camp is almost destitute.

" Monday, May 19th. We made an early start this morning, steering our course as yesterday, six miles west, and encamped on the side of the mountain. . . . The travelling some better than it was back, although we have hills and brush to encounter yet. We encamped about six miles from the ocean, where we have a fair view of it.

"Tuesday, May 20th. As our horses were lame and tired, we concluded to remain here and let them rest, and kill and dry meat, as elk appeared to be plenty from the sign. After breakfast myself and Mr. Virgin started on horse back for the sea shore, following an Indian trail that led immediately there. After proceeding about five miles west, we found we could not get any further on horse back along the Indian trail; so we struck out from the creek that we had followed down, and about three miles from where we first struck it. After leaving the creek with some considerable difficulty, we ascended a point of steep and brushy mountain that runs along parallel to the seashore, and followed that until we could get no further for rocks and brush. We got within eighty or one hundred yards of the beach, but being pretty much fatigued, and not able to ride down on account of rocks and brush, we did not proceed any further in that direction. . . . On our return we saw some elk. I went after them, and Mr. Virgin stayed with the horses. I did not get to fire 'on them, and saw a black bear and made after him, and shot and wounded him very badly, and heard Mr. Virgin shoot and call me to come to him. I made all the haste I could in climbing the mountain to where Mr. Virgin was. He told me that some Indians had attacked him in my absence, shot a number of arrows at him and wounded the horses. . . . I rested a few minutes and proceeded on cautiously to the place where we had left the horses, and found an Indian lying dead and his dog by him. Mr. Virgin's horse had two or three arrows in him, and he lying down. We got him up and made camp a little before night.

"Wednesday, May 21st. Still at the same camp. . . . The timber in this part of this country is principally hemlock, pine, and white cedar, the cedar trees from five to fifteen feet in diameter. The underbrush is hazel, oak, briars, currants, gooseberry and Scotch-cap bushes, together with alder, and sundry other shrubs too tedious to mention. The soil of the country is very rich and black, but very mountainous, which renders the travelling almost impossible with so many horses as we have.

"Thursday, May 22nd. All hands up early and preparing for a move. Had the horses driven to camp and caught ready for packing up, and it commenced raining so fast that we concluded to remain here today, as we could not see to direct our course for fog along the mountains. We have not seen or heard any Indians since the 20th, when Mr. Virgin killed the one that shot at his horse. Oh, God, may it please Thee, in Thy divine providence, to still guide and protect us through this wilderness of doubt and fear, as Thou hast done heretofore, and be with us in the hour of danger and difficulty as all praise is due to Thee and not to man. Oh, do not forsake us, Lord, but be with us and direct us through."

For nearly two weeks thereafter the party wandered about the rugged country, seeking a way down to the coast; and more than once they found it necessary to turn back over hard-won miles because of some impassable barrier. During this time they were forced to kill their "last dog" for food, as they were "entirely out of provisions with the exception of a few pounds of flour and rice."

Finally on June 8th they managed to reach the ocean near the mouth of the Klamath River, and camped on the beach. Henceforth they kept to the coast, sometimes riding at the very lip of the surf, sometimes swinging a mile or so inland. Now and then the deep and yawning mouth of a stream made it necessary to build rafts. Game was somewhat more plentiful now; and various articles of food, such as camas root, clams, dried fish and berries, were bought with beads from the Indians, who generally displayed rather more fear than friendliness, and sometimes risked a sneaking hostility. On the 23rd of June the party crossed the 42nd parallel, the northern boundary of the Mexican country.

Under date of July 2nd Rogers tells us that " as the most of the men's times expired this evening, Captain Smith called all hands and gave them up their articles, and engaged the following men to go on with him until he reaches the place of deposit, viz: John Gaiter, Arthur Black, John Hanna, Emanuel Lazarus, Abraham La Plant, Charles Swift, Thomas Daws, Toussaint Mari-shall.   Daws' time to commence when he gets well enough for duty.   Also Peter Ranne and Joseph Palmer, at the above named price, one dol-lar per day, and Martin McCoy two hundred dollars from the time he left the Spanish country until he reaches the deposit."

On the 4th of July, so Rogers tells us, " Mari-shall caught a boy about ten years old and brought him to camp.   I gave him some beads and dried meat.   He appears well satisfied."

Still pushing northward along the coast, on July 11th the party reached the Umpqua River, and camped near a village of Umpqua Indians, who seemed altogether friendly.   The last two entries made by Rogers in his diary run as follows:

" Saturday, July 12th.   We commenced cross-ing the river early and had our goods and horses over by eight o'clock, then packed up and started a northeast course up the river and travelled three miles and encamped.   Had several Indians along. One of the Indians stole an ax and we were obliged to seize him for the purpose of tying him before we could scare him to make him give it up. Captain Smith and one of them caught him and put a cord around his neck, and the rest of us

stood with our guns ready in case they made any
resistance.   There were about fifty Indians present, but they did not pretend to resist tying the
other.   The river at this place is about three
hundred yards wide and makes a large bay that
extends four or five miles up in the pine hills. . . .
We traded some land and sea otter and beaver fur
in the course of the day.   Those Indians bring
Pacific raspberries and other berries.

" Sunday, July 13th, 1828. · We made a pretty
good start this morning, directing our course
along the bay east, and travelled four miles and
encamped.   Fifty or sixty Indians in camp again
today.   We traded fifteen or twenty beaver skins
from them, some elk meat and tallow, also some
lamprey eels.   The travelling quite miry in
places.   We got a number of our pack-horses
mired, and had to bridge several places.   A considerable thunder shower this morning, and rain
at intervals through the day.   Those Indians tell
us after we get up the river fifteen or twenty miles
we will have good travelling to the Wel Hamett
or Multinomah, where the Callipoo Indians live."

While writing these words — the last he would
ever write — Rogers must have felt that his
earnest prayers had been answered.   The " Wel
Hamett or Multinomah " was the Willamette
River.   A day or two of easy travel, and they
would be in the valley of that stream with a good
trail leading northward down to the Columbia

and the great post of the Hudson Bay Company, Fort Vancouver. Both by trapping and through trade with the natives they had, in spite of their hardships, accumulated a large amount of beaver fur during their long northward journey through a virgin wilderness; and though they were still far from their comrades under Sublette and Jackson, the unknown country had been passed, and henceforth they would travel by river valleys all the way to the headwaters of the Snake, where the main body would be waiting. Doubtless it was a merry company that camped on the north bank of the Umpqua that night of July 13th, 1828.

Early the next morning, Smith, as had been his habit, started afoot up the river to find a good trail for his party, " the country being very swampy in the lowlands and woody in the mountains." One account states that he went alone; another, that he went with " a little Englishman " and an Indian; a third, that he was accompanied by two of his party and one Umpqua. Strict orders were given that no Indians should be admitted to the camp during his absence; but scarcely had he disappeared up river when the order was disobeyed. The penalty for disobedience was swift and terrible.

On July 12th, it will be remembered, Smith had dealt rather roughly with the Indian who had stolen an ax. This man, who happened to be a chief, now seized the opportunity to avenge his wounded dignity. At a signal from him the Indians, outnumbering the little band three to one, attacked the unsuspecting trappers. Effective resistance was out of the question. Fifteen of the white men went down at once under the knives of the Indians. Only two of those in camp escaped — Black and Turner. At the moment when the signal for attack was given, Black, who seems to have been out of the crowd, had just cleaned and loaded his gun. Three Indians leaped upon him, but he succeeded in shaking them off; and seeing his comrades down and fighting hopelessly, he fired into the mass of Indians and fled into the heavily wood country to the north. Turner, a very large and powerful man, was serving as cook that day. Having no weapon within reach when the savages fell upon him, he snatched a burning stick from the fire, knocked down four of his assailants, and ran up stream in the direction taken by Smith, whom he met returning at some distance from the camp. Turner was under the impression that he was the sole survivor of the camp; and, realizing the impossibility of coping with their numerous enemies, these fled together up the Umpqua and across the divide to the Willamette. Black, in the meanwhile, was following the coast northward, convinced that he alone had escaped.

In his Autobiography, Dr. McLoughlin, factor of Fort Vancouver on the Columbia, gives the following account of the affair [1]: "One night in August, 1828, I was surprised by the Indians making a great noise at the gate of the fort, saying that they had brought an American. The gate was opened, the man (Black) came in, but was so affected he could not speak. After sitting down some minutes to recover himself, he told us he was, he thought, the only survivor of eighteen men conducted by Jedediah Smith. All the rest, he thought, were murdered. . . . Broken down by hunger and misery, as he had no food but a few wild berries which he found on the beach, he determined to give himself up to the Killimour, a tribe on the coast of Cape Lookout, who treated him with great humanity, relieved his wants and brought him to the fort, for which, in case whites might again fall in their power, and to induce them to act kindly to them, I rewarded them most liberally. But as Smith and his two men might have escaped, and, if we made no search for them, die at daybreak the next morning, I sent Indian runners with tobacco to the Willamette chiefs to tell them to send their people in search of Smith and his two men, and if they found them, to bring them to the fort and I would pay them, and telling them if any Indians hurt these men we would punish them, and immediately equipped a strong party of forty well-armed men. But as the men were embarking, to our great joy Smith and his two men arrived.

[1] Clarke. "Pioneer Days of Oregon History."

" I then arranged as strong a party as I could make to recover all we could of Smith's property. I divulged my plan to none, but gave written instructions to the officer, to be opened early when he got to the Umpqua, because if known before they got there, the officers would talk of it among themselves, the men would hear it and from them it would go to their Indian wives, who were spies on us, and my plan would be defeated. The plan was that the officer was, as usual, to invite the Indians to bring their furs to trade, just as if nothing had happened. Count the furs, but as the American trappers mark all their skins, keep these all separate, give them to Mr. Smith and not pay the Indians for them, telling them that they belonged to him, that they got them by murdering Smith's people."

As a result of this expedition sent out, " from a principle of Christian duty," by Dr. McLoughlin, Smith recovered most of his peltry, which he sold to the Hudson Bay Company, receiving therefor a draft on London for $20,000. Some of the horses of the ill-fated party were also returned, together with a few articles of personal property, among which was the diary of Harrison G. Rogers which we have been quoting.

In order to appreciate the magnanimity of Dr. McLoughlin, it must be remembered that the firm of Smith, Jackson and Sublette was then coming to be regarded as a somewhat dangerous competitor; and considering the manner in which the Americans had relieved Ogden of a fortune in furs during the spring of 1825, a lesser man than McLoughlin might have seized this opportunity to enjoy the discomfiture of his rivals.

In his " Pioneer Days of Oregon History," S. A. Clarke, who knew McLoughlin, has left us the following tribute to this fine old gentleman: " Over six feet in height, powerfully made, with a grand head on massive shoulders and long snow-white locks covering them, he was a splendid picture of a man. The Indians knew him as the White Eagle, and they respected him as they never did anyone else. . . . He was a convert to Catholicism, and in no sense was he a bigot or lacking in the Christian charity that recognizes true effort with good will wherever it is met. . . . His policy to effect peace with the Indians was potent for good. . . . With his grand manner and majestic port, heightened by white, waving hair, he was the embodiment of power and justice. . . . He was indeed, as he was styled, ' the Czar of the West.' His rule was imperial for a thousand miles, and his mere word was law. Yet there was a genuine beneficence in his nature that overcame the pride of life and the lust of the flesh, and made him the special providence to open the Canaan of the Occident to the Civilization of the East."

XXI

THE END OF THE TRAIL

DURING the absence of Jedediah Smith, the main body of trappers under Sublette and Jackson had been working in the upper Snake River country, and in the fall of 1828 they returned to Great Salt Lake for the winter. Shortly afterward, Sublette started for St. Louis with the furs, travelling by way of South Pass and the Platte. He reached his destination about the middle of December, 1828, and in March, 1829, began the return journey to the mountains with sixty men and a train of supplies. He ascended the North Platte to the Sweetwater, thence heading for the Popo Agie, a southern tributary of the Wind River, where the summer rendezvous was to be held. Reaching the appointed place about July 1st, he found there a greater portion of the band that had wintered at Salt Lake. Jackson had remained with a small party west of the Great Divide.

According to Joseph Meek, who made his first trip to the mountains that year, the rendezvous lasted until about the first of August. " In this period," says Meek, " the men, Indian allies, and

other Indian parties who usually visited the camp
at this time, were all supplied with goods. The
remaining merchandise was adjusted for the convenience of the different traders who should be
sent out through all the country traversed by the
company. Sublette then decided upon their
routes, dividing up his forces into camps, which
took each its appointed course, detaching, as it
went, small parties of trappers to all the hunting
grounds in the neighborhood." [1]

Sublette himself now set forth to find Smith,
who had agreed to meet him on the upper waters
of the Snake River. He pushed up the Wind
River, crossed the mountains and entered the
valley now called Jackson's Hole, after the partner whom he found encamped there. For some
time Sublette and Jackson waited at this point
for Jedediah Smith. Finally growing uneasy,
Sublette sent small parties out in various directions to search for the missing partner. One of
these bands wandered into Pierre's Hole, " an
emerald cup set in its rim of amethystine mountains," and there, with but four men — one of
whom was Arthur Black — Smith was found trapping along the streams of the beautiful valley.
He had spent the winter of 1828–29 at Fort Vancouver as the guest of the venerable Dr. Mc-
Loughlin; and in March he had resumed his journey toward the place of rendezvous, ascending

[1] Victor, *op. cit.*

the Columbia to a point near the big bend, thence striking out north and east to Flathead House, from whence, turning southward along the route he had followed with Ogden in the winter of 1824–25, he had reached Pierre's Hole.

We are told that there was great rejoicing over the finding of Smith; and well might this be, though it is doubtful if the importance of what this man had accomplished was thoroughly understood by his comrades. His had been the first overland party of Americans to reach California; he had been the first white man to travel the central route from Salt Lake to the Pacific, and the first to traverse the full length of California and Oregon by land. Of the thirty-two men who had shared in his adventures, twenty five had been slain by the Mohaves and the Umpquas. During three years of wandering west of the Rockies, he had covered fourteen degrees of latitude and eleven degrees of longitude. It was one of the greatest of Western explorers that Sublette's men found trapping in Pierre's Hole that summer of 1829 — and he was then but thirty one years old!

During his sojourn with Dr. McLoughlin at Fort Vancouver, Smith, by way of showing gratitude for the generosity of his host, had agreed that the firm of which he was a member should henceforth confine its operations to the country east of the Great Divide. Accordingly, after spending the balance of the summer in Pierre's

Hole, the three partners crossed over to the head-waters of the Madison Fork of the Missouri. During the fall and early winter of 1829, the various parties of the firm worked the country lying between the sources of the Missouri and Yellowstone, finally going into winter quarters on the Wind River. While the camp was celebrating Christmas, William L. Sublette and Black Harris, with a few dogs to carry their blankets and supplies, started on snow-shoes for St. Louis. Sublette took with him a letter from Jed Smith to his brother, Ralph, of Ashtabula, Ohio, urging the latter to come west.

Shortly after the departure of Sublette and Harris, the party on the Wind River, finding the pasturage there insufficient for the horses, moved to the Powder River. After much wandering and many stirring adventures during the spring and early summer of 1830, the party moved back to the valley of the Wind River, where the rendezvous of that year was to be held.

On the 10th of July, Sublette arrived with eighty-one men mounted on mules, ten loaded wagons drawn by five-mule teams, two dearborn buggies, a milch cow, and twelve head of steers — the latter having been driven along as an insurance against famine until the buffalo country should be reached. The wagons and buggies brought out by Sublette that year were the first to trundle up the great natural road soon to be known as the Oregon and California Trail.

The Wind River rendezvous of 1830 was the last ever held by the firm of Smith, Jackson and Sublette; for in the first week of August the business was sold to a new firm, called The Rocky Mountain Fur Company, and composed of Thomas Fitzpatrick, Milton G. Sublette (a brother of William L.), Henry Fraeb, Jean Baptiste Gervais, and James Bridger.

Immediately after the sale, Smith, Jackson and Sublette began the journey to St. Louis, with one hundred ninety packs of beaver, worth about $80,000. Reaching the city in October, 1830, Jed found his two brothers, Austin and Peter, awaiting his arrival, Ralph having been unable to leave home.

At that time the golden era of the Rocky Mountain fur trade was nearing its end, and more and more the adventurous spirits of the frontier were becoming interested in the overland traffic with Taos and Santa Fé, New Mexico. Until the beginning of the 19th century, New Mexico had received all its imported goods from Vera Cruz over a long and difficult trail; but early in the century American merchants had begun to realize the fact that goods could be transported more cheaply to New Mexico by way of the Missouri River and the Great Plains than from any Mexican port. In 1804 one Morrison, a merchant of the old French town of Kaskaskia, succeeded in sending a pack-train of merchandise to Santa Fé, but lost the profits of his venture through the dishonesty of his agent. Other merchants followed the example of Morrison, but none attained any conspicuous success during the next seventeen years.

Josiah Gregg, the principal authority on this unique phase of westward expansion, tells us that the Santa Fé trade may be dated from the year 1821 when " Captain William Becknell of Missouri, with four trusty companions, went out to Santa Fé by the far western prairie route." [1] This band started from Franklin, a town on the Missouri River two hundred miles above its mouth. " Notwithstanding the trifling amount of merchandise they were possessed of," says Gregg, " they realized a handsome profit "; and thereafter the trade with Santa Fé increased rapidly. In 1822 the value of merchandise transported westward across the prairies and the deserts was $15,000; in 1824, $35,000; in 1825, $65,000; in 1827, $90,000; in 1828, $150,000; in 1831, $250,000! Up to the year 1823, pack-animals alone were used. In 1824, wagons were employed for the first time; and after 1826 all traffic was by wagon.

It will be remembered that when Jedediah Smith first landed in St. Louis, the great period of the fur trade was just beginning, and men

[1] Gregg. " Commerce of the Prairies."

talked of little else than the fortunes that could be realized in that romantic industry. Eight years had passed since that time, and now the Santa Fé trade was the talk of the town. Smith, in company with his brothers, Peter and Austin, and his partners, Sublette and Jackson, decided to engage in this new business.

On April 10th, 1831, the Smith party, consisting of eighty five men, started from St. Louis with twenty two loaded wagons and a six-pound cannon. Travelling up the valley of the Missouri River, they met Thomas Fitzpatrick near Lexington. He was returning to St. Louis from the Yellowstone country, but was easily persuaded to accompany his old comrades to Santa Fé.

Near the last of April the party reached the town of Independence, which, though but four years old, had already come to be the point of rendezvous for the Santa Fé traders, as well as for the Rocky Mountain trappers. Formerly the town of Franklin, one hundred eighty seven miles down stream had been the point of departure; but with the founding of Independence in 1827, the latter place was found to be more convenient, being the westernmost settlement on the Missouri, a stream that was navigable for at least eight months during the year and offered a cheap and easy means of transportation from St. Louis.

On the 4th of May, 1831, the wagon train of Smith, Jackson and Sublette moved out from In-

dependence on the road to Santa Fé with seven
hundred seventy five miles of prairie wilderness
ahead. The first point of importance reached
after leaving the border was Council Grove, one
hundred fifty miles out — a wooded valley lying
along a branch of the Neosho River. Here it
was customary for the westbound parties to halt
for the purpose of electing officers, deciding upon
the order of march, agreeing as to the rules that
should be obeyed, and defining the duties that
should be performed by each member.

Josiah Gregg, who started with a caravan for
Santa Fé just eleven days after the departure of
Smith's party, has left us a vivid account of the
organization and personnel of these parties:
" One would have supposed," he writes, " that
electioneering and party spirit would hardly have
penetrated so far into the wilderness; but so it
was. Even in our little community we had our
office seekers and their political adherents, as
earnest and devoted as any of the modern school
of politicians in the midst of civilization." When
a " Captain of the Caravan " had been elected,
the business of organization began. " The pro-
prietors were notified by proclamation to furnish
a list of their men and wagons. The latter were
generally apportioned into four divisions. . . .
To each of these divisions a lieutenant was appointed, whose duty it was to inspect every ravine
and creek on the route, select the best crossings,

and superintend what is called, in prairie par-
lance, the forming of the caravan. . . .

" The wild and motley character of the caravan," continues Gregg, " can be but imperfectly
conceived without an idea of the costumes of the
various members. The most fashionable prairie
dress is the fustian frock of the city-bred merchant, furnished with a multitude of pockets
capable of accommodating a variety of ' extra
tackling.' Then there is the backwoodsman with
his linsey or leather hunting shirt — the farmer
with blue jean coat — the wagoner with his flan-
nel-sleeve vest — besides an assortment of other
costumes which go to fill up the picture.

" In the article of fire-arms there is also an
equally interesting medley. The frontier hunter
sticks to his rifle, as nothing could induce him to
carry what he terms in derision ' the scatter gun.'
The sportsman from the interior flourishes his
double-barrel fowling piece with equal confidence
in its superiority. The latter is certainly the
most convenient description of gun that can be
carried on the journey, as a charge of buckshot
in night attacks (which are the most common)
will of course be more likely to do execution than
a single rifle-ball fired at random. . . . A great
many were furnished beside with a bountiful supply of pistols and knives of every description.

" At the Council Grove the laborers were employed in procuring timber for axle-trees and

other wagon repairs, of which a supply is always
laid in before leaving this region of substantial
growths; for henceforward there is no wood on
the route fit for these purposes; not even in the
mountains of Santa Fé do we meet with any
serviceable timber. The supply procured here is
generally lashed under the wagons, in which way
a log is not infrequently carried to Santa Fé, and
even sometimes back again." [1]

Final preparations having been made at Council Grove, the caravan began the journey in earnest. Gregg tells us that when the nature of the
country would permit, it was customary to march
in four columns, and he remarks that a caravan
proceeding in this manner " presented a very fine
and imposing spectacle." In making camp for
the night, or in case of attack by Indians during
the day, the wagons were thus easily placed in the
most advantageous position for defence, the exterior columns swinging outward and then meeting, the two inner columns falling back and wheeling outward to form a quadrangle with the first
two ·columns. Into the corral thus formed the
animals were driven, thus rendering a stampede
impossible, while, protected by the hollow square
of heavily loaded wagons, the men were enabled
to render a very good account of themselves in
case of a scrimmage.

The caravan of Smith, Jackson and Sublette

[1] " Commerce of the Prairies."

pushed forward rapidly, reaching the Ford of the
Arkansas River, three hundred ninety two miles
west of Independence, in about three weeks.
Thus far no considerable difficulties had been encountered; and though they had lost one man,
who had strayed away from the main body and
been killed by Pawnees, they had every reason to
be in the best of spirits, for they had now covered
slightly more than half the distance to Santa Fé.

However, they were now about to enter upon
the most difficult stage of the whole journey.
After crossing the Arkansas, the route led for a
distance of over sixty miles across a region of
utter desolation to the forks of the Cimarron
River. "This tract of country," says Gregg,
" may truly be styled the grand prairie ocean; for
not a single landmark is to be seen for more than
forty miles — scarcely a visible eminence by which
to direct one's course. All is as level as the sea,
and the compass was our surest as well as our
principal guide."

Before entering this desert, it was customary to
lay in a good supply of water. Smith and his
comrades seem to have neglected this precaution,
hoping, doubtless, to find occasional water holes;
but the summer of 1831 was unusually dry, and
no water holes were found. Within two days
after striking out from the Arkansas, the party
began to experience the tortures of thirst and the

famished animals began to die.   Confused by a
maze of buffalo trails that led nowhere, taunted
and misled by lying mirages, Smith and his comrades struggled onward.

We will let Josiah Gregg tell the rest of the
melancholy story.   He had it from a Mexican
buffalo hunter, who, in turn, had been told by
the Comanche Indians, themselves protagonists in
the final act of the tragedy: " In this perilous
situation, Capt. Smith resolved at last to pursue
one of the seductive buffalo paths, in hopes it
might lead to the margin of some stream or pond.
He set out alone; for besides the temerity which
desperation always inspires, he had ever been a
stranger to fear; indeed he was one of the most
undaunted spirits that had ever traversed the
Rocky Mountains. . . . But, alas! for unfortunate Capt. Smith! After having so often
dodged the arrow and eluded the snare of the
wily mountain Indian, little could he have thought,
while jogging along under a scorching sun, that
his bones were destined to bleach upon those arid
sands! He had already wandered many miles
away from his comrades, when, on turning over
an eminence, his eyes were joyfully greeted with
the appearance of a small stream meandering
through the valley that spread before him.   It
was the Cimarron.   He hurried forward to slake
the fire of his parched lips — but imagine his dis-

appointment at finding in the channel only a bed
of dry sand! With his hands, however, he soon
scratched out a basin a foot or two deep, into
which the water slowly oozed from the saturated
sand. While with his head bent down, in the
effort to quench his burning thirst, he was pierced
by the arrows of a gang of Comanches, who were
lying in wait for him! Yet he struggled bravely
to the last; and, as the Indians themselves have
since related, killed two or three of their party
before he was overpowered."

Thus, on the 27th of May, 1831, died Jedediah
Strong Smith at the age of thirty three. No
monument marks the spot where this great Western explorer met his end. His bones were picked
by the wolves and crows and left to bleach in the
arid bed of the Cimarron until the next freshet
should bury them in the sands.

At winter quarters on the Wind River in December, 1829, Smith had written as follows to his
brother Ralph; and no man who knew him
ever questioned his sincerity: " It is that I may
be able to help those who stand in need that I
face every danger. It is for this that I pass over
the sandy plains, in heat of summer, thirsting for
water where I may cool my overheated body. It
is for this that I go for days without eating, and
am pretty well satisfied if I can gather a few
roots, a few snails, or better satisfied if we can
afford ourselves a piece of horse-flesh, or a fine

roasted dog; and most of all it is for this that I deprive myself of the privilege of society and the satisfaction of the converse of my friends! "

Let his own words be his epitaph.

LIST OF SOURCES

Dale, H. C. The Ashley-Smith Explorations and the Discovery of a Central Route to the Pacific. Cleveland. The Arthur H. Clark Co. 1918.

Chittenden, H. M. The American Fur Trade of the Far West. New York. Francis P. Harper. 1902. 3 vols.

South Dakota Historical Society Collections. Vols. I and III.

Flint, Timothy. Recollections of the Past Ten Years. Boston, 1826.

Howe, Henry. Historical Collections of the Great West. New York and Cincinnati, 1857.

Solitaire (John S. Robb). Major Fitzpatrick, Discoverer of South Pass. St. Louis Weekly Reveille, March 1st, 1847.

Smith, J. S. Letter to General Clark, written at " Little Lake of Bear River, July 17th, 1827." In Kansas Historical Society MSS. Given in full by Dale.

Rogers, Harrison G. Journals describing portions of both journeys of Smith to California. Missouri Historical Society MSS. Dale presents these for the first time.

Ashley, William H. Letter to General Atkinson, written at St. Louis, Dec. 1, 1825, describing the winter journey from Fort Atkinson to Green River and the descent of Green River. Missouri Historical Society MSS. Given in full by Dale.

Smith, Austin. Letter to his father, written at " Walnut Creek on the Arkansas, three hundred miles from the settlements of Missouri, Sept. 24, 1831." Gives account of the death of J. S. Smith. Kansas Historical Society MSS.

Smith, J. S. Letter to his brother, Ralph, written at Wind River, Dec. 24, 1829. Kansas Historical Society MSS.

Gregg, Josiah. The Commerce of the Prairies. New York, 1845. Reprinted in Thwaites' Early Western Travels, vols. XIX and XX. Cleveland, 1905.

Maximilian, Prince of Wied-Neuwied. Travels in the Interior of North America. London, 1843.

Clarke, S. A. Pioneer Days of Oregon History. Portland, 1905. 2 vols.

Richman, I. B. California under Spain and Mexico. Boston, 1911.

Bonner, T. D. The Life and Adventures of James P. Beckwourth. New edition edited by Godfrey Leland. London, 1892.

Dodge, Major General G. M. Biographical Sketch of James Bridger. New York, 1905.

Victor, F. F. The River of the West. Hartford, 1870.

Encyclopedia of St. Louis, 1899.

The Western Monthly Review. Cincinnati, 1830. Vol. III.

Laut, A. C. The Conquest of the Great Northwest. New York, 1908. 2 vols.

Parker, Rev. Samuel. Journal of an Exploring Tour Beyond the Rocky Mountains. Ithaca, 1844.

Ruxton, G. F. Life in the Far West. Edinburgh, 1887.
————— Adventures in Mexico. London, 1847.

Sage, R. B. Rocky Mountain Life. Boston, 1847.

Farnham, T. J. Travels in the Great Western Prairies. New York, 1843.

Coutant, C. G. History of Wyoming. Laramie, 1899.

Wyeth, J. B. Oregon, etc. Cambridge, 1833. Reprinted in Thwaites' Early Western Travels, vol. XXI. Cleveland, 1905.

Hodge, F. W.   Handbook of American Indians.   Washington, 1912.   2 vols.

Ogden, G. W.   Letters from the West, etc.   Reprinted in Thwaites' Early Western Travels, vol. XIX.   Cleveland, 1905.

Bullock, W. A.   Journey through the Western States, etc.   Reprinted in Thwaites' Early Western Travels, vol. XIX.   Cleveland, 1905.

Bryant, W.   What I Saw in California.   New York, 1849.

Irving, Washington.   Astoria.

————————— Captain Bonneville.

Cook, P. St. G.   Scenes and Adventures in the U. S. Army.   Philadelphia, 1857.

THE END